RIVER
PHOENIX

RIVER PHOENIX
HERO & HEARTTHROB

GRACE CATALANO

BANTAM BOOKS
TORONTO • NEW YORK • LONDON • SYDNEY • AUCKLAND

GRACE CATALANO is the author of the popular biography *Kirk Cameron: Dream Guy* (Bantam) and *Teen Star Yearbook* (Paperjacks). She is the editor of the popular teen magazine *Dream Guys* and has interviewed and written about scores of celebrities. She and her brother, Joseph, wrote and designed *Elvis—A 10th Anniversary Tribute* and *Elvis and Priscilla*. Grace lives with her family in Valley Stream, New York.

RIVER PHOENIX: HERO & HEARTTHROB
A Bantam Starfire Book / October 1988

The Starfire logo is a registered trademark of Bantam Books, a division of Bantam Doubleday Dell Publishing Group, Inc. Registered in U.S. Patent and Trademark Office and elsewhere.

ISBN 0-553-27728-6

Published simultaneously in the United States and Canada

Bantam Books are published by Bantam Books, a division of Bantam Doubleday Dell Publishing Group, Inc. Its trademark, consisting of the words "Bantam Books" and the portrayal of a rooster, is Registered in U.S. Patent and Trademark Office and in other countries. Marca Registrada. Bantam Books, 666 Fifth Avenue, New York, New York 10103.

PRINTED IN THE UNITED STATES OF AMERICA

O   0 9 8 7 6 5 4 3 2

To the four of us

CONTENTS

1

THE YEAR OF RIVER PHOENIX

Far from Hollywood, in the jungle of Belize, Central America, the humidity is high, mosquitoes are biting, and the sun is beating down on the cast and crew of *The Mosquito Coast*. Most young Hollywood stars might have difficulty adjusting to these harsh working conditions. But not River Phoenix.

Unlike his peers, River grew up in Venezuela and lived in such places as Mexico and Puerto Rico before he was even seven years old. His large family includes his mother, Arlyn, his father, John, and four younger siblings, Leaf, Rainbow, Liberty, and Summer. Even though they traveled from country to country and experienced some very hard times, River's childhood memories are good ones.

Remembering those days, he sighs. "We were very poor. A lot of people made fun of us because we were always traveling and living out of the back of a VW my dad made into a camper."

River's alternative was to enter show business so he could help his parents pay the rent. He began working in television at the age of nine and has since skyrocketed to become the top young actor in movies.

Now eighteen years old, River Phoenix is a handsome young man with deep bluish-gray eyes and a shock of dark blond hair. Critics have praised him as "The Most Exciting Teenage Actor of the 1980's" and "Hollywood's Hottest Young Star." *The Mosquito Coast* director Peter Weir says of River, "He has the look of someone who has secrets. The last time I remember seeing it in someone unknown was with Mel Gibson." In December 1987, River won his first Youth-in-Film Award as Best Young Male Movie Star.

He's had starring roles in everything he's ever done, including the hit films *Explorers, Stand By Me, The Mosquito Coast, A Night in the Life of Jimmy Reardon,* and his newest movies, *Little Nikita* and *Running On Empty*. He is an intense young actor with powerful screen presence. There are other impressive teenage stars on and off the screen, but there is only one River Phoenix.

He is adored by young girls who look up to him and idolize him. He receives hundreds of fan letters every day and is on the cover of every major teen magazine. His talent is extraordinary—he became a major movie star in a very short span of time, and many film producers now bombard him with scripts. But even though he's been in the public eye since the age of nine, there is much more to River than anyone has ever known.

What is the secret behind River's remarkable success? He'd tell you part of it is originality. Instead of studying other actors' techniques, River relies on his own intuition and innate talent. His techniques are really quite simple.

"I hate the 'actory' way of saying things," he explains. "When I do a scene, I just try to be in the scene's reality. I try to forget everything I've done and be as simple as possible. In simplicity, there is truth."

River must be doing something right because audiences will laugh with him and cry with him. He makes his characters come to life and leaves a lasting impression on the audience long after the movie's credits roll up.

But River also feels part of his success has been his good fortune in playing great roles. He admits that teenage actors have been given the opportunity to play more meaningful characters in the last few years. That's why, he feels, there is such a surge of younger actors in movies and on television.

"There are more young characters being written in movies so there are more young actors hired to play the characters," he says. "I guess that's because with kids there's a certain freshness that people like.

"Actually there have always been teen actors," he continues. "It's just that there are more of us now, and we're better at it because the roles are not just the clichés of young people."

River is careful about which roles he will accept and which he will refuse. "I am actually a strong personality and I would never do anything unless I believe in it," he reasons. He feels that acting is a great creative outlet because it gives him the chance to portray another person's life. When River is engrossed in filming, he actually becomes his character even after the cameras stop rolling.

"I walk, talk, even dream like the person I'm playing," he says. "You can't be yourself. If you are, then it's not good for the filming because you're living someone else's life. I don't like being around people that I know really well or things that remind me of me."

Perhaps the reason why River is such a good actor stems from the fact that he's very serious about each role he undertakes. He actually puts his own life on hold while he's working on a movie. He does admit that he likes to play different roles for the experience and the challenge of displaying his acting abilities.

"Whenever I wanted to live a more ordinary life, I'd get a part that called for an ordinary kid," he reflects. "I learned so much. In a way, acting's like a Halloween mask that you put on."

That may be true, because in the romantic comedy *A Night in the Life of Jimmy Reardon,* River played a character completely different from his own personality. "The only thing we shared is that we look alike," he muses.

Although he's received accolades for his wonderful performances, it has taken River a while to get used to watching himself on-screen. "He doesn't like anything he's done," says his mother. "He's only just starting to like himself in *Stand By Me.*"

With six movies already under his belt, River Phoenix, at eighteen, is a movie star in every sense of the word. Yet he'll often explain that he hates the fact that a label has been placed on him.

He doesn't think of himself as a movie star at all. "I don't like the word star—movie or rock," he asserts. "I know I'm in movies but I don't want to be known as a movie star."

River Phoenix the actor is somewhat different from

River Phoenix the young man. There is an allure of mystery surrounding him, and he remains secretive about his life and career. Who is he really? Where is he from? Is there something he's trying to hide?

Millions of River's fans keep asking these kinds of questions about the hero they adore. Stepping out of character, River Phoenix, the serious-minded young superstar, describes himself as "a normal guy doing a job." What he still doesn't realize is that he is taking the acting world by storm—and there's no stopping him now!

2

CHILDHOOD, FLOWER POWER, AND THE RIVER OF LIFE

On August 23, 1970, River Jude Phoenix was born in a cozy log cabin in Madras, Oregon, to thunderous applause. "That's exactly how it was," recalls his mother, Arlyn. "River came out to a roar of clapping and cheering."

His parents chose not to have their baby in a hospital; instead their newborn arrived the old-fashioned way with friends gathered in the small room to watch the birth. As unusual as that may seem, River's early childhood was just as unconventional. His parents were sixties-style free spirits who found work as missionaries for religious groups in places such as Venezuela, Puerto Rico, and Mexico.

"I'm glad I didn't have a traditional upbringing," explains River modestly. "I think I'm a better person for it. Having lived through all those experiences made me a better actor, too."

When he talks about his parents, he boldly remarks

that it was fate that brought them together. And he just may be right.

Geographically, the young secretary from Manhattan would never have crossed paths with the part-time gardener/carpenter from California. They were living two completely different lives in two different states. But as River explains, "It's very interesting that my mom and dad met at all. I feel they were meant to be together."

Born in the Bronx, New York, his mother, Arlyn Dunetz, married very young and got a job working as a secretary in New York City. On the outside, Arlyn seemed content, but in reality she was restless, unhappy, and clearly wanted more out of life.

In 1968, she impulsively quit her job, terminated her first marriage, and set off on her own to seek a happier existence. With very little money in her pocket, she hitchhiked from New York to California and there she met John.

He was a strikingly handsome man who had also been married before and was the father of a baby girl named Jo Dean. John, who was a high-school dropout, had been involved in a serious car accident at age sixteen that left him partially disabled. When Arlyn met him, he was supporting himself through carpentry and gardening.

Whatever John's last name was before he changed it to Phoenix has never been known. John chose Phoenix at a time when the family desperately needed help. It was a symbol of hope that they would rise above their rough times, as the mythical phoenix rose from its own ashes.

It was this kind of philosophy that brought John and Arlyn together. Although it seemed, at first, that the two were worlds apart, they quickly discovered that they shared many of the same interests. With the United States involved in the Vietnam War, they both were searching for peace in the midst of troubled times.

The couple fell in love and in less than a year they were married. Together they would begin a new life, one that was devoted to love and the beauty of nature around them. After drifting from state to state, the couple joined a commune in Madras, Oregon, in late 1969. They lived a simple life there until their first child, River, was born.

During the day, John moved irrigation pipes in mint fields; at night they read passages from the spiritual book *Siddhartha,* by Hermann Hesse. The book, which is about the river of life, affected them in a profound way, and they decided early on that their first son would be named River.

"The name is gentle and earthy, just like River himself," says Arlyn. When he began acting, River would constantly have to answer the question, "Is River Phoenix your real name or something made up for show biz?" When he'd reply, "It's real," the next curiosity from reporters was, "Why did your parents give you such an unusual name?" To which, River has answered countless times, "My parents were flower children and intense nature lovers. They didn't want their children to have regular names like everyone else."

Even as a little boy, River was more serious than other boys his age. "I don't know," he offers. "I was always a very curious kid. I'd spend most of my time thinking of questions to ask, then I'd ask them."

His father remarks, "River was born grown-up," and his mother says with a smile, "River was always a leader.

He's been a good example to others. His seriousness really helped him down the line."

River spent the first seven years of his life traveling with his parents to different states and countries, but he wasn't alone for very long. By the time he was one, a baby girl was born to John and Arlyn while the family was living in Crockett, Texas.

In keeping with their tradition of unusual but beautiful names, their first baby daughter was called Rain. John and Arlyn would continue to give their children names that would "remind people of the beauty around them," says Arlyn. "But our children know they can change their names at any time to whatever they want."

With this in mind, Rain, at age eleven, found her name to be "a little drab." She decided to change it to Rainbow, which she feels is cheerful and vivacious.

Unfortunately, John and Arlyn didn't find their life in Texas fulfilling spiritually or emotionally. John couldn't find work and Arlyn wanted to see other countries outside of the United States.

The Phoenixes made the spontaneous decision to uproot their two small children and travel to Puerto Rico. When they arrived, they found it to be a wondrous place and exactly what they were looking for. It was in Puerto Rico that their third child, Joaquim Rafael (later changed to Leaf), was born in 1974.

"Joaquim (pronounced wah-keem) is a Spanish name," says Arlyn. "We loved it because we had been living in Puerto Rico and we were really becoming one with the people there. But then when Leaf got older, he would say, 'Why do I have this name Walking?' He thought it was w-a-l-k-i-n-g because his brother was River and his sister was Rain. We just told him he could change it if he wasn't comfortable with it."

Leaf eventually chose his own name. "When I was about five years old, my dad and I were out raking leaves," he remembers. "It was sort of a unanimous decision to change my name to Leaf."

The Phoenixes called Puerto Rico their home for two years. It was at this time that John and Arlyn taught their children the importance of having solid values. They always believed that love, beauty, and nature were more important than money, and they passed those beliefs on to River and his siblings. Even though John and Arlyn lacked in material things, a wealth of love flowed from them to their children.

"Arlyn and I have always been full of faith and we love everything," confides River's dad. "We tried to pass that on to our kids, and I think they've all learned it pretty well."

In Puerto Rico it seemed like the Phoenixes were finally settled. River remembers those days vividly. "I have a very good memory," he explains. "I remember everything that has ever happened to me. I even remember falling off my bike when I was three and living in Puerto Rico."

River, who was quite an active kid, acquired his nickname Rio (Spanish for "river") while living there. He made friends and enjoyed playing in the golden sunshine every day.

But one day, his parents announced that they'd be moving again. With three little mouths to feed, John and Arlyn kept finding themselves deeper and deeper in debt and the time seemed right to change their surroundings. As missionaries passing along the word of God, they headed for South America. They lived in several cities before settling in Caracas, Venezuela, where River's folks became archbishops for the Children of God cult. It was a religious group they strongly believed in at the time.

Those few years in Venezuela proved to be the hardest of River's life. "I've been through some pretty desperate times," he reveals, almost hesitantly. "I've lived a lot even though I'm still young. But I feel that when you're born into a way of life—and that's all you know—you don't mind it. The good times and the bad are all part of the experience."

Later, River would say that life in Venezuela was both stimulating and exasperating. Times may have been tough for the family, but the Phoenixes never lost faith. If anything good resulted from those years, it was that they learned to share everything with each other.

"We've always relied on each other's strengths," observes River. "We've always been real close. Even at the worst times, we didn't get depressed. We kept saying, 'This will work out.' We've always been very positive."

At age five, River was an adorable, blond-haired boy with a passion for sports and an interest in music. "I started singing because my parents did and I was always around it," he says.

River sometimes had trouble falling asleep, and he would be soothed by his mother's voice singing the song "You've Got A Friend." It wasn't long before he learned the words to the song and was singing it, too. Even at this young age, River showed his creativity. He decided when he was five that he wanted to learn to play an instrument and make his own music.

Without the benefit of music lessons, River would

teach himself how to play the guitar, bass, and piano by the time he was ten years old. It began with a Christmas gift in 1975 that changed his life.

Christmas 1975 was a happy time for the Phoenix family. They had become close with many of the people in Venezuela, including Spanish singer Alfonso Sainz, who River would talk to for hours about music. He was very impressed by him because Alfonso was a working musician—something River dreamed of eventually becoming.

The singer's Christmas gift to River that year was a guitar. When he gave it to him, the young boy's face broke into a wide smile, and he didn't let the guitar out of his sight for a minute. He'd practice the different chords and notes every day, and within a few months, he was able to play a complete song.

River devoted all his spare time to the guitar and began writing his own songs at age six. He thought that if he learned enough songs, he would be able to play them in the streets and get money to help his family pay the rent and buy food for dinner. As soon as he saw the money running low, he and his sister, Rainbow, would go down to the street and sing and play the guitar.

"We did it because we needed money, but we also wanted to pass along love. That was something our parents taught us," says River, recalling those early days.

People passing the two talented performers showed their appreciation and gave them money, which they immediately gave to their parents. River and his siblings have never known the meaning of selfishness. Even though he and Rainbow earned the money by themselves and could have bought anything they wanted with it, it went directly into the family's savings.

River cared about his family and the world around him. His love for animals resulted in the sudden decision to stop eating meat. It wasn't long before the rest of his family agreed with him and also became vegetarians.

"I stopped eating meat when I was five," says Rainbow. "The reason I do it is for the animals."

The Phoenixes have a philosophy of harmlessness, so they don't eat meat or take from animals in any way. They consume no milk or milk products, and use no soaps that have animal products in their ingredients.

The Phoenixes only eat vegetables, fruit, grains, and soy products. Their recipes come from a book called *The Cookbook for People Who Love Animals,* which includes such dishes as tofu cheesecake and whole wheat spaghetti.

Arlyn, who decides what her family should and shouldn't eat, says, "Sprouts are perfect food with all the chlorophyll. We originally started this as an experiment because River wanted us to and now it makes so much sense."

In 1976, another baby was born to this loving family. The birth took place on Liberty Day in Venezuela, and John and Arlyn poetically christened their fourth child Libertad Mariposa (later changed to Liberty Butterfly) in honor of the day she was born.

The year also saw changes in River and Rainbow, who were fast becoming a popular brother-and-sister performing act, and they appeared on a South American television show. Although their performing started out as just a way to help their parents with money problems, it was really the first sign of things to come for the talented Phoenix kids.

Arlyn comments today, "I always had a vision that

our kids could captivate the world. I feel like they are headed in that direction."

With so much interest in music, six-year-old River never thought acting would be the career he would pursue first. But deep down inside, he felt that the music business was a hard field to break into.

He spent every available minute practicing the guitar and piano, and he began developing songwriting skills as well. "I remember when he was a little guy," says his mother. "He was very conscientious about writing music and wouldn't go out and play until he was finished arranging a song on his guitar."

Soon River and Rainbow were asked to play in a concert in Caracas with the ballad singer Jose Luis Rodriguez. This kind of exposure was very exciting for River. However, his music career had to end as it became increasingly impossible to continue living in Venezuela.

On August 23, 1977, River celebrated his seventh birthday. There was no cake or party for him. Instead, he spent the day in a hut, eating coconuts and mangoes that fell off the trees.

Today, he still shudders when he thinks of it. "It was disgusting," he recalls. "It was a shack, it had no toilet and was rat-infested." With conditions going from bad to worse, John and Arlyn knew it was time to move on.

The Children of God cult was steadily changing, and the Phoenixes felt the group had abandoned its original principles. They no longer agreed with its new beliefs. They desperately wanted to get their children out of Venezuela and away from the group.

They knew it would only be a matter of time before they could flee the country, but they had no money for

travel expenses, and no one had offered them any help
—yet.

River remained calm and unshaken throughout this sudden turn of events. He knew his family had overcome bad times before and they'd get through them again. Just when it seemed like they'd never get out of Venezuela, another missionary got the family passage on a freight ship headed for Florida. The Phoenixes were once again searching for the peace and happiness they still hadn't found.

3

THE SCHOOL OF HARD KNOCKS

"I hope people don't just focus on the hard times we had because there were really good times, too," said River Phoenix during a recent interview.

In 1977, those bad times seemed to be a thing of the past for the Phoenix family as they tried to get their lives back in some order. Disillusioned with the Children of God cult, they fled Venezuela in such a hurry, they left many of their personal possessions behind. River was the only one to take his guitar with him on the journey back to the United States.

It was during this difficult time that John took the name Phoenix. It gave them strength in knowing that although they were down, they would rise again.

And they did.

The family settled near Arlyn's parents in Winter Park, Florida, where John started his own landscaping business. "I worked fourteen to fifteen hours a day," he says. "And Riv and the kids would help me out, carrying sod and things like that."

River also continued singing and writing songs on his guitar, and he and Rainbow performed in several local amateur contests. These months were very productive for the family because they marked the beginning of important changes that would take place in less than one year.

While in Florida, River's youngest sister, Summer Joy, was born. A beautiful baby, Summer was the last child born to John and Arlyn. The family, now consisting of seven members, was ready to tackle the future.

Because they couldn't afford much, the Phoenixes lived in a small house. In the confinement of a few rooms, there was very little privacy for River; and even though he'd sometimes wake up in the middle of the night to hear the baby crying, he really didn't mind it. After all, he and his brother and sisters were extremely close and did everything together. Because of all the moving around, none of the Phoenix kids had any friends outside of the family. Their attitude toward one another was "one for all and all for one."

River spent his days in Florida working with his father and being tutored by his mother; his nights were spent rehearsing new songs he wrote with Rainbow. It was at this young age that River decided he wanted to enter show business full time.

When he started winning some of the talent contests he entered, the ambitious young boy decided to ask his parents what they thought. "My parents didn't push me into it. They never even thought about it," he says. "I went to them and told them I wanted to help. I figured

I'd play the guitar and sing with my sister, and we would be on television the next day."

Although he would be on television in less than a year, he wouldn't be playing the guitar right away and it wouldn't happen overnight. But River was realistic. He knew he'd have to work hard at his career and he was ready for the challenge.

"I used to tell people I wanted to change the world and they used to think, 'This kid's really weird,'" recalls River, who now feels he had a bit of an arrogant attitude. "I'm not saying, 'case closed,'" he adds with an earnest grin. "It's just that I always wanted to touch people by entertaining them. That's really the only way I know how."

He and Rainbow continued to perform at many amateur contests in Florida, and they were so talented that an article was written about them in a local newspaper. A friend of the family's sent the article to actress Penny Marshall, who at the time was starring as Laverne on the TV show *Laverne and Shirley*.

But before she read it, the article fell into the hands of an employee at Paramount Studios, who contacted John and Arlyn and invited them to visit if they were ever in Los Angeles.

River's parents saw this opportunity as a sign toward better times and they decided to move to California permanently. Although this spur-of-the-moment decision seemed risky, John remembers, "I said to myself, 'What a crazy person you are.' But the stars were so bright, I felt it was right."

He gave up his landscaping business, packed the Phoenixes' belongings into their Volkswagen van, and the family began its adventurous trip to California.

Because John had turned the van into a camper, the seven Phoenixes plus the family dog spent day and night in the car. "Things went wrong for us all the time," says Arlyn. "One night it was freezing, but we didn't have a back window in the camper. It got so cold, we stuffed Pampers in the window."

Remembering that night, her younger son, Leaf, adds, "We huddled up against the dog for warmth."

Fame and fortune waited down the road for River and his family. But, for now, the future star was in for a bumpy ride. As they got closer and closer to California, River couldn't wait to arrive and begin working in show business. By this time, he had decided to put his musical career on hold to pursue work as an actor. He felt there was a bigger calling for actors in Hollywood and he longed to be part of it.

"I remember we'd roll into gas stations in our beat-up car and I'd tell the attendant, 'I'm going to be an actor,'" he reminisces.

River's dream would soon become a reality. When the Phoenixes arrived in California, they settled in Los Angeles. Arlyn found work as a secretary at NBC Studios and John stayed home to tutor the kids. In his entire life, River has only spent a few months in public school. His parents have taken the responsibility for their children's education. Later, a tutor would be hired to travel with River on the sets of his movies; but in the beginning, his parents taught him academics, spirituality, and ethics at home. John and Arlyn always felt it was important for one parent to be home at all times. With Arlyn working all week at NBC, John found himself taking part-time jobs as a gardener on weekends. For former flower children, this new lifestyle took a while to adjust to, but they didn't want any more changes. This time they wanted to succeed.

From the moment the family arrived in California, River had his mind set on becoming an actor, and it didn't take Arlyn long to get the ball rolling in that direction. As a secretary at NBC Studios, she was able to find out just when auditions were being held for television commercials. When it came time to send in a group of kids to read for these sixty-second spots, Arlyn made sure River was included.

The auditions were nerve-racking and time-consuming for the young hopeful. There were so many other kids auditioning that competition was fierce, and River wondered how he would ever be the one chosen for a part.

But the spunky youngster had the look most casting agents were searching for. He was blond, charismatic, and had the kind of boundless energy that television audiences would find appealing. That is, if he got the job.

His first bit of disappointing news was that, although he fit the casting agent's description and read his lines perfectly, River did not win the first commercial he auditioned for.

Luckily, neither River nor his mother took the rejection seriously. He feels very fortunate to have had the support of his family behind him throughout the beginning of his career. He has said that without their encouragement and love, he never would have had the stamina to chase the dream he wanted so badly. The frustrations can be so great that some child actors would give up all together. River, however, persisted.

"In the beginning, it's just hard to get anywhere," he

recollects. "You're constantly going, but you're spinning your wheels, sliding down the hill. You climb back up, then slide down again. Then after a while, it's almost like an escalator or an elevator and from then on it takes you right up."

Although River kept hoping to be "discovered" and become a star, four years would lapse before he got on that elevator taking him to the top. As a newcomer, he had to work hard and hope for the best. With a growing interest in show business, Arlyn decided that the logical thing to do was to find an agent for River. She contacted the Screen Actors Guild and made an appointment to see Iris Burton.

From the moment River walked into her office, Iris knew she would be able to find work for him. Known in Hollywood as a superagent, she had a reputation for shaping the careers of young unknown actors. Her list of clients reads like a who's who of the hottest young stars, with River and fellow teen heartthrob Kirk Cameron at the top.

Iris has a keen eye for talent and predicted right from the start that River was going to be a big star. At the age of nine, he possessed both charisma and energy—two qualities she looks for in potential actors. She signed him immediately and explained that she would start him in commercials.

"I start all the kids off in commercials," she says. "That's to get them familiar with cameras. They have to learn how to sustain eight hours on the set. That is the best way to get into the business. If they do well in commercials, I try to move them into theatrical."

Working under the guidance of Iris, River soon won his first commercial and plunged into the career he'd always dreamed of. With success just around the corner, the Phoenix family realized that their gamble on California was going to pay off. It almost seemed as if River was born to be an actor, because even at the age of nine, he generated excitement on-screen.

He was the "kid" in commercials for Ocean Spray, Saks Fifth Avenue, and Mitsubishi and he probably would have gone on to become a very successful "commercial kid." But at the age of ten, after just a few months of acting, River decided to quit commercials for good.

His reason was unusual and interesting. It was a decision that could have cost him the career he was working so hard at, but it didn't. "Commercials were too phony for me," he says. "It was selling a product, and who owns the product? I mean, are they supporting apartheid? I just didn't like the whole thing. Even though it helped us pay the rent."

As an up-and-coming young actor gaining experience and television exposure, River was very brave to give it all up. He wasn't worried, though, because he knew that if he tried hard enough he would eventually win roles he believed in.

For one year, he tried out for small parts as the kid in large families, but found no work. Then, he decided to turn his attentions back to his first love—music.

Ironically, it would be his music that would eventually help him break into television. When his agent found out he sang and played the guitar, it opened new doors for River. Now he wasn't just a young actor; he had other talents too. And those talents helped him get his first big break on the small screen.

Once again, he and Rainbow began singing together. They'd rehearse River's new songs for hours. They found that the more they played, the better they were beginning to sound. When River's agent called to say she'd arranged an audition with a television show called *Fantasy*, it was a dream come true. She told River they were looking for a child who could sing and she thought he would be perfect.

Fantasy was a variety show that utilized the talents of everyday people. Each week there were three guests scheduled who would live out their "fantasies" on the air. Since young River was really hoping to someday enter the music business, he was thrilled to get the opportunity to sing and play his guitar on television. When the producers found out that River sang duets with his sister, they thought it would be great to have them perform together on the show.

Appearing on American television for the first time, River couldn't believe he was getting paid to do what he loved most. The experience was very exciting for the young duo and made them both realize that show business was definitely going to be part of their futures.

Although River wanted to break into movies someday, he liked working on television. Over the next few years, he would play a string of impressive television roles that would establish him as one of the hottest young actors in Hollywood.

4

RIVER PHOENIX TAKES FLIGHT

For three years, River Phoenix worked steadily on television. Following his brief stint on *Fantasy,* he won a role in *Seven Brides for Seven Brothers* as Guthrie, the youngest of the brothers. The short-lived television series gave River the opportunity to further display his singing talent as well as his acting abilities.

The show, like the 1954 MGM musical movie of the same name, was a western with music. River played his guitar and sang with the rest of the cast every week.

During the filming of *Seven Brides for Seven Brothers,* River observed everything that went into the production. He's always been interested in learning as much as he can while working on a set. He's the kind of actor who asks a lot of questions and isn't satisfied until he gets every one answered. He liked watching himself on-screen, in the beginning, because he learned from it. He was constantly correcting little flaws he noticed about his performance. After a few shows, the young talent seemed very relaxed in his role and was beginning to catch attention from audiences.

One day while he was rehearsing his lines, he received a package from the studio. It was filled with a small stack of fan mail addressed to him. He'd never received a fan letter before and couldn't believe that someone actually would write to him. He read every letter and answered every one. Things had certainly happened fast for River. He felt that he was really on the right road to success after all.

Just as River was soaring to stardom, he learned the crushing news that *Seven Brides for Seven Brothers* had been canceled after only twenty-two episodes. After starring each week on television, River found himself back at square one. The next few months were devoted to auditioning again, a task quite difficult to resume.

At first, losing roles was a harrowing experience for River, but he quickly learned not to think about the rejections. "When I didn't get a part I auditioned for, I'd say, 'Oh, well, something better will come along,'" he says, nonchalantly. "That's the attitude you've got to take."

With a loving family behind him, River never felt discouraged. But the Phoenixes were still in financial trouble. Arlyn's job at NBC didn't pay enough to support the family, and John was having a hard time finding work. River felt responsible for helping his family and it made him very ambitious.

Thinking back, he professes, "Just wanting to have some money so that we could live comfortably was an incentive to pray a lot for parts."

His determination finally paid off when he won roles in two television miniseries, *Celebrity* and *Robert Kennedy: The Man and His Times.*

In the latter, River portrayed the well-known politician as a boy. Although he only appeared in the first fifty minutes of the docudrama, his performance made a strong impact on many producers. By the time he was thirteen years old, he was already a three-year veteran of television. He guest-starred on TV shows such as *Family Ties, Hotel,* and *It's Your Move,* but he didn't really find his niche in show business until 1984.

On March 7 of that year, River starred in an Afterschool Special called *Backwards: The Riddle of Dyslexia.* He nabbed the much-coveted role of Brian Ellsworth in the critically acclaimed one-hour special, the first serious drama he would star in.

River's sensitive portrayal of the young boy suffering from an undiagnosed case of dyslexia helped audiences understand this reading disorder. After the special aired, River was never again hired for comedic roles.

Instead, he was cast in the dramatic TV movie *Surviving: A Family In Crisis,* which tackled the subject of teen suicide. The two-hour movie starred such highly respected actors as Ellen Burstyn, Marsha Mason, Len Cariou, Paul Sorvino, Molly Ringwald, and Zach Galligan. It dealt with a teenage couple's suicide pact and the effect it had on their families. *Surviving* was probably the strongest drama River ever appeared in. His performance was superb and the movie proved to be a real training ground for the young thespian.

By playing such challenging roles, River was able to prove his abilities as an actor. When he first entered show business, acting was just a means to help his family pay bills, but soon it became a very big part of his life. For the Phoenixes it was a fairy tale come true.

In just three years, River was living a real-life rags-to-riches story. Yet with all that had happened to him in such a short time, he was only concerned with proving to the world that he was talented and could play any role. He'd been lucky, because with his roles in *Backwards: The Riddle of Dyslexia* and *Surviving: A Family In Crisis,* he knew he was being given the chance to improve.

Although River spent hours at a time on television and movie sets, he felt fortunate to always have one member of his family with him. Even now, his parents try not to let River go on location alone.

He has always appreciated the support he's received from his close-knit family. "When I'm working on a set, I see a lot of people who don't have anybody in their lives," he confesses. "Oh, they have superficial friends, but that doesn't count. Every night they go back to their hotel rooms alone. I never want that. I'm glad somebody from my family has always been with me."

As a young boy plunging into the acting world, River has always felt the need to go over his lines numerous times before having to stand before the cameras and act. This kind of dedication to his craft has resulted in what many critics predict will be a very long and successful career for River.

Although he now likes to suggest how he should play his scenes, it was different when he first started acting. He watched the directors and listened to them very carefully. He's always felt that a director is very important on the set of a show or movie and that it is necessary to listen to what one had to say. "I guess I was more vulnerable to directors who were set in their ways when I was younger," he says.

Looking back on his first three years in show business, the amount of work River did was astonishing even to him. He'd played a wide variety of roles, from comedy to strong drama, and he felt it was a good beginning to what he was hoping would be a steady career as an actor.

At thirteen, River was looking forward to moving into feature films, but he hadn't mentioned it to anyone yet. Then one day his agent phoned to tell him about an open call for a new movie titled *Explorers*. River didn't know it then, but this one audition would be the beginning of his flourishing movie career.

5

THREE KIDS AND A SPACESHIP

When the auditions for *Explorers* were announced, teenage actors from everywhere poured into the open calls. Executive producer Mike Finnell, who initiated a nationwide search in Los Angeles, New York, San Francisco, Chicago, and Texas, was looking for newer faces as opposed to established child stars.

As the auditions dragged on, Finnell wasn't having much luck "discovering" a new star. He knew what he wanted, but the right actors were taking longer to find than he had anticipated.

River Phoenix was the first actor to impress Finnell enough to be called back. The casting director had met young River and was completely taken with him. She contacted Finnell and told him she thought he'd be perfect as one of the young heroes in *Explorers*. After numerous call-backs and a screen test, River was cast in the leading role of Wolfgang Muller. He couldn't believe that in his very first film, he was cast as one of the stars, instead of in a supporting role. It was a dream come true for River, but what made the experience even more exciting was that the movie was a fantasy-adventure.

River considered *Explorers* to be "really unique and a movie kid's dream. I got a thrill just from reading the script," he marvels.

Explorers centers around three best friends who have very different personalities. Besides River's character, Wolfgang, who is the scientist of the group, there's Ben Crandall (Ethan Hawke), the daydreamer and commander, and Darren Woods (Jason Presson), the mechanic. Together they construct a spaceship out of old parts they find in a junkyard, like a TV set, two washing machine doors, and the body of an old Tilt-a-Whirl ride from a long-defunct carnival. Their spaceship is named *Thunder Road* (after a song on Bruce Springsteen's classic *Born to Run* album) and the three adventurers take it into space.

Their quest leads them to a grand starship where they encounter two teens from outer space named Neek and Wak. After getting to know the aliens, Ben, Wolfgang, and Darren discover that life in space is very much like life on Earth. It is a moving story about kids growing up and fulfilling fantasies.

The movie also starred Amanda Peterson (*A Year in the Life*) as Ben's girl friend, Lori Swenson, and veteran Hollywood actor Dick Miller as Charlie Drake, the helicopter pilot who discovers the explorers' spaceship.

With the key roles cast, producer Edward S. Feldman was enormously pleased with the chemistry between River, Jason, and Ethan. "We've got the combination of the right kids who work well together," he said. "We were very careful—it's hard to find three kids that an audience will want to look at for two hours."

Mike Finnell echoed Feldman's words and added, "They've become their roles to a certain extent. The Darren Woods character is kind of an outsider and Jason is like that. Wolfgang Muller is all over the place and very hyper and River is definitely like that. And Ethan is Mister Regular Guy. So, they are very much like their roles."

While Finnell saw a similarity between River and his character, Wolfgang Muller, River felt just the opposite. Wolfgang donned horn-rimmed glasses and spent his time working in his science laboratory in his basement. The young actor found he had to put a lot of energy into every scene. "Every time they said, 'Action,' I had to really work hard," he remembers. "I feel that it gave me more experience in acting. It gave me a chance to throw a little comedy in because *Explorers* was a fantasy."

He has said that because Wolfgang was such a different role for him, he had the most fun *becoming* his character. To prepare for the role, River carefully thought about what this nerdy genius kid would be like beyond the script. That was the only way River felt he would be able to make Wolfgang believable on film.

"You have to do that if you're really going to create the role and put all you have into it," he explains. "You must try to figure out how Wolfgang would live. So, I thought about what his financial situation is. Like are his parents middle class, upper class, or lower class. What kind of clothes he wears. If he likes girls or school. I tried to create his character. I did it the way I saw."

Eric Luke, who wrote the screenplay for *Explorers,*

had a very definite idea of what Wolfgang Muller was supposed to be like. "When I was growing up, I had a friend who was Wolfgang," he says. "Like in the movie, he actually had parents who were research scientists and Wolfgang was a really scientific kid. I remember I went over to his house because he had a great comic book collection."

Luke used his vivid memories of his own boyhood friend to create Wolfgang Muller in *Explorers,* but River had his own way of playing the role. "The Wolfgang in the script and the way they visualized him wasn't exactly the way I played him," he says. "It was the main idea. But if it didn't change, as the character did in the movie, then it wouldn't be a full-of-life character. Towards the film's end, we've all grown up in many ways. We've explored different areas of the world and space, and we've learned a lot. And I did as an actor. When little personality traits go into the character, given by the actor, that adds life to the character."

Explorers was directed by Joe Dante, whose previous credits included *The Howling, Piranha,* one segment of *Twilight Zone—The Movie,* and the enormously popular *Gremlins.* River looked up to Dante all through the production of *Explorers.* "I honestly didn't know how this movie was going to work out," River admits. "I didn't know Joe when I was auditioning. It was after I got the part that I met him. He was really great. I had never worked with a director whom I'd gotten so close to before."

Dante was pleased with River's performance and had nothing but praise for the young talent. He allowed River to voice his opinion on his character and change things he thought were necessary. During filming, Dante didn't stop rolling the cameras. There were many scenes where River and the two other boys ad-libbed and Dante captured those priceless moments on film. Later he used most of the footage. "We've gotten some very good things on film from these kids," he said. "Sometimes, they say things that no writer would ever think of because very few fourteen-year-olds write movies."

Most of *Explorers* was shot on the huge Paramount Pictures studio sound stages under tight security. On October 15, 1984, principal photography began in picturesque Petaluma, California, and then the crew moved indoors. The movie would take five long months to complete, with final filming on the special-effects sound stage of Lucasfilm's Industrial Light and Magic facility in San Rafael. Most of River's key scenes were shot on Paramount Sound Stage Eight, which housed the spectacular set for the spaceship and the interior of the alien ship.

The nickname given to this particular set was Funhouse so no one outside of the crew knew anything about the story. One strict rule on the set was that no secrets would be revealed to the public before *Explorers* was released.

When River first arrived on the set of the Funhouse, he heard a terrible sound echoing through the stucco sound stage. It turned out to be the Brobdingnagian boilers in each corner of the stage. The noise resulted from tons of dry ice being boiled into white vapor, which was needed for the suspenseful scenes.

The special-effects scenes fascinated River. "They were fun to watch," he says. "The special effects were incredible. I was really interested in the dry ice and the hydrogen they use."

River would learn the patience needed during scenes that didn't satisfy the director and had to be shot over and over again. One scene that stands out in his mind took place on the Funhouse set. He was seated in the cramped quarters of the spaceship with Ethan and Jason. They were waiting for a signal from Joe Dante. As more and more white vapor flooded the set, Dante shouted, "Action," and the three boys started to climb out of the spacecraft.

Ethan and Jason ascended and the scene seemed to be going smoothly until River climbed out. When his face was in camera range, his oversize glasses had fallen off and dangled from one ear. Dry-ice fog rose around River as he heard Dante shout, "Cut. Get back inside the ship. We'll do another take right away."

That scene was shot so many times that Dante later said, "We shot as much film on that one scene as I shot on my entire first movie." But finally, after numerous takes, both Dante and River were satisfied.

Another sound stage was devoted to the Earth junkyard where the explorers find the old parts to build their spaceship. On this location, Dante shot all his night scenes. Since the child labor law didn't permit River, Ethan, and Jason to work at night, this indoor sound stage was a tremendous advantage for the crew. Inside the security of the Paramount lot, they were free to light the set so it looked like a real outdoor location at night.

Working with child stars posed a few more problems for Dante. Since his young stars were only able to work four hours a day, the movie had to be shot completely out of sequence. They started with the end, then went back to the beginning and the middle, and completed with the end.

During the five months, River, Jason, and Ethan were growing and the costume people had to keep letting out their clothes. When filming began, Jason was the shortest member of the cast. By the end of the movie, he had grown four inches and was almost taller than Joe Dante. Working so closely with the three young stars, Dante was impressed at how they were able to juggle filming with doing their four hours of required schoolwork every day. There was a tutor present on the set to ensure their daily education.

"I don't know how they did it," says Dante, referring to River, Ethan, and Jason's tough schedule. "I mean they had to go to school and take tests. The only difference is that for them recess is when we made our movie. So recess was actually working."

Because the cast and crew were together for hours every day, occasional arguments did erupt between the fourteen-year-olds, but they were quick to overlook their disagreements. The truth was, they were having loads of fun filming the movie and they didn't want anything to spoil that fun.

"It's just that when you're with someone for five months, and when you hang out with them constantly, five days a week, sometimes you can get on each other's nerves," River explains. "We really got along exceptionally. I mean, we did have our little disputes, but they were nothing."

River found he had more in common with Ethan than Jason and spent more time with him during breaks. One day, the two boys wandered to the video unit located on one side of the studio. The takes of the day were filmed on videotape so the cast and crew could review the day's scenes.

Although River and Ethan flicked on the television, they weren't interested in viewing their scenes that particular day. Instead, they changed channels to catch a few minutes of MTV.

While the rest of the cast and crew puttered around the set, Dante glanced over at River and Ethan, who were completely engrossed in MTV. Dante walked over to see what his two young stars were watching.

He sat down next to them and said, "Ah, come on guys. Let's change channels."

River moaned, but let his director scan through the channels. Dante stopped at an old Abbott and Costello film and watched a few minutes before noticing that River and Ethan had begun talking. He smiled, then sighed. "Okay. Back to MTV," he said, and switched the channel to a video of Billy Idol singing in a bathroom shower.

River was soon singing along with the rock star, and as Ethan joined in, too, their director walked away muttering something about the "generation gap."

River has said that the cast and crew of *Explorers* was like one big happy family. "Working with Ethan and Jason was like having foster brothers you move in with for a while and get to know. They were very easy to work with. There are some Hollywood kids who are really brats and it's just hard to deal with them. I've been lucky that I haven't been such a brat. I'm trying my best not to be. It has been hard because when we get hyper on the set, sometimes we get on the adults' nerves. And there were times we got tired of just hanging around the set."

River didn't have too many days like that. Every day on the set of *Explorers* was a new adventure for him. Of all the scenes, he says his favorites are the ones that included special effects. "There was this one scene with a slide and we were supposed to fall down a chute in the spaceship," he recalls. "That was so much fun, because we got to do it over and over again for different camera angles."

River also remembers the day Eric, the cameraman, went down the slide in front of him facing upward, and he was facing down, looking right into the camera lens. With scenes like those, River felt grateful to be part of such an exciting movie.

Explorers was released in July 1985 during a time when Hollywood was churning out teen-oriented science-fiction and fantasy films. Since the 1982 classic *E.T.* was such a blockbuster, producers felt the need to cast teenagers in fantastic settings. The early and middle 1980's saw such films as *Gremlins, The Last Starfighter, The Goonies,* and *Back to the Future,* just to name a few.

In fact, *Gremlins* was such a hit for Joe Dante and producer Steven Spielberg that it was rereleased the same month that *Explorers* was released. Fortunately for the director, he didn't feel any direct competition between his two films. "The only way I would've felt competition was if *Gremlins* was rereleased before *Explorers*. But the new film was out five weeks before *Gremlins,* so it was all right," he said.

Explorers garnered good reviews, but did even better with the teen crowd. Because of its success, there has been talk of an *Explorers* sequel, but so far nothing has materialized.

Even though it is unlikely that River would have the time to repeat his role, he has summarized what he thinks his character might be like in part two. "Wolfgang is in his own little scientific world," he begins. "So I think that what he's striving for is to be a well-known scientist when he gets older. He wants to be honored by many people. He has a great deal of dignity and I think that, sometimes, he just thinks he's always right. Wolfgang is different. He was really a very interesting character to play."

When production wrapped, River returned to his quiet existence of playing his guitar and going on auditions. With summer only a few months away, River began thinking ahead. Every summer he had earned his extra money mowing lawns, but somehow he felt that the summer of 1985 would be different. Maybe it was because he knew that when *Explorers* was released in July more people were going to know him. He waited, wondering what exciting thing would happen next in his life.

One day, while River was playing football in his yard with his brother and a few friends, his mother called him in. "Iris just called," she said. "She wants you to try out for a role in a new movie."

"What is it?" River asked, curiously.

Arlyn walked over to the telephone, where she picked up a piece of paper she had scribbled some information on. "All she said is that it's based on a short story by Stephen King," said Arlyn. "She thinks you're perfect for one of the lead roles and the working title is *Stand By Me*."

Before River knew it, he was on a plane headed for Oregon to begin working on the movie that would be his ticket to success.

6

STAND BY ME

There is a turning point in every successful actor's life; the time when a promising beginner becomes an established movie star almost overnight. When River Phoenix went to test for *Stand By Me*, he didn't realize it would be the turning point in his life and career.

River was the first actor to be cast in *Stand By Me*. During his screen test, he projected natural acting abilities that immediately impressed director Rob Reiner. Without a single professional acting lesson behind him, River convincingly played the scene handed to him. He possessed raw talent and the intensity Reiner was looking for, and it only took a few call-backs before he was convinced River was perfect. River Phoenix won the pivotal role of Chris Chambers in the movie that would catapult him to superstardom.

"*Stand By Me* was my acting class," he says. "I was learning something new and different every day."

The movie is based on *"The Body,"* a novella from

Stephen King's book *Different Seasons*. King, the author of popular horror novels such as *Carrie* and *The Shining*, loosely based this story of four friends on his own childhood experiences.

Set in the fictional town of Castle Rock in the summer of 1960, a twelve-year-old budding writer named Gordie Lachance (Wil Wheaton) is about to begin an extraordinary two-day trek into the Northwestern forest with his best friends—Chris Chambers (River), Teddy DuChamp (Corey Feldman), and Vern Tessio (Jerry O'Connell).

While playing a penny card game in their tree house, they find out that a twelve-year-old boy, who has been missing for days, was struck by a train and killed. Fascinated, the four friends wager that if they can be the ones to discover the body and report it, they could take all the credit. In the eyes of the people of Castle Rock, they will be known as heroes.

As the boys bravely set out along the railroad tracks, their adventure begins innocently with the dream of becoming town heroes. But it quickly turns into a journey of self-discovery. Before the long trek is over, Gordie, Chris, Teddy, and Vern will be tested in ways they had never imagined.

Rob Reiner, best known for his Emmy Award-winning role as Archie Bunker's "meathead" son-in-law, Mike Stivic, on the TV series *All in the Family*, was no stranger to youth-oriented films. He directed the hit films *This is Spinal Tap* and *The Sure Thing*, and he brought a special sensitivity to *Stand By Me*.

At the time, he had been looking for a new challenge and decided Stephen King's story was perfect. "The characters were very strong and very well-drawn," he explains. "For me, it became more than just four boys searching the woods for a body."

River was immediately drawn to this touching script. He knew it was going to be an important film, but admits he never expected it to be the sleeper hit of 1986. The story of four boys coming of age in a small town, combined with elements of suspense, adventure, and comedy, was exactly the type of film he was searching for.

Playing Chris, River was able to stretch his acting abilities to new heights. Whereas Wolfgang Muller in *Explorers* is a conservative, scientific genius, Chris is a tough-on-the-outside, sensitive-on-the-inside protector and leader. He is smart, but has been told he isn't. He worries about his future because, with a juvenile-delinquent brother and an alcoholic father, he is convinced Castle Rock will never let him rise above his family's reputation.

"Chris wants so bad to climb above it all," says River, describing his character. "He's known in the town as that no-good Chambers kid. I really felt sorry for him."

River's warmth for the role carried over into his portrayal. His enthusiasm burned strongly throughout the production. Although preparing himself for scenes took long hours of concentration, the skilled young actor managed to step into his role with ease.

"It's weird," he explains. "When you're in a movie like *Stand By Me* and you're in those scenes, it's not like you're filming a movie. Even though they say 'Action' and 'Cut.' You're not thinking that it's all going to be on film, nor do you really care. I think that's what makes a good performance."

Movie audiences not only fell in love with River, but

also with the other three outstanding actors. Brown-haired Wil Wheaton, who was born on July 29, 1972, began acting at age seven when he won his first television commercial for Jell-O Pudding Pops opposite Bill Cosby. After that, the ambitious go-getter won a string of roles in TV movies *A Long Way Home* and *Young Harry Houdini,* and full-length feature films *The Buddy System, The Last Starfighter,* and *The Farm.*

But it was the role of Gordie, the fledgling writer in *Stand By Me,* that had the most effect on him. "I knew it was a good film," he says sincerely. "But I never expected it to receive so much critical acclaim."

He was so inspired by his character that he actually began writing short stories in his spare time. "I picked it up while I was researching my role and never stopped," he explains. "I basically write mysteries and horror stories like my favorite author, Stephen King."

Wil, who is now one of the series regulars on *Star Trek: The Next Generation,* discovered the meaning of friendship during that carefree summer he spent filming *Stand By Me.* "We did a lot of stuff in Oregon like having water-gun fights and shooting off fireworks," he says enthusiastically. "But the thing I've learned was how important friendship really is. I think we all felt that way and that's why we've kept in touch. River is one of my best friends and I like to get together with Corey and Jerry whenever we have some time."

Corey Feldman is no stranger to the business of performing. He was just three years old when he fell in love with acting. He made his feature-film debut in *Gremlins* and followed it up with *Friday the 13th: The Final Chapter.* It wasn't until he starred as Mouth in *The*

Goonies, however, that he began to think of acting as a career.

"Before *The Goonies,* I just considered acting a game," says Corey, who was born on July 16, 1971. "But as roles became more difficult, I became more serious about how to play them."

Out of all the roles he's played, Corey admits his favorite character is Teddy in *Stand By Me* "because it was the biggest challenge of my career." He enjoyed working with director Rob Reiner, who he found to be very patient and helpful.

"In the movie, my character has this hideous-sounding laugh," says Corey. "For a long time Rob and I worked on how we could do it. We tried twenty-five different laughs before finally settling on one."

Corey, who won a Youth-in-Film Award for his performance in *The Lost Boys,* is the star of four new films, *License To Drive, Long Before Tomorrow, Money From the Sky,* and the sequel to *The Goonies.* He loved working with River and remarks, "River is really cool! He loves the macho image!"

Rounding out the *Stand By Me* foursome was newcomer Jerry O'Connell. "I was the youngest of the four and the only one from New York," says Jerry, who is best known for his work in dozens of television commercials.

"The other guys in *Stand By Me* had at least heard of each other before," he continues. "But no one knew me; that was my first big movie. In the beginning, I was really scared. But it didn't take me long to start feeling comfortable around River, Corey, and Wil."

As River and his fellow costars delved deeper into

their roles, all four boys became their characters that summer. "There was a small part of each of us in our roles," reflects River. "There had to be for it to work. The one part I really had in common with Chris was that he was the peacemaker of the group. But aside from that, I wasn't anything like him."

The movie didn't go overtime or overbudget. In fact, things went so smoothly during the production that it was relatively uneventful. So River, Wil, Corey, and Jerry decided to have some good old-fashioned fun of their own. Their on-screen rowdiness often manifested itself off-screen.

Wil Wheaton remembers all the fun and games. "You set four kids loose and give them X amount of money a week to do whatever they want—I guess we *did* go a little crazy," he admits with a grin.

Going "a little crazy" is putting it mildly. The quartet literally invaded the motel where they stayed. If they weren't throwing parties in the pool or devising count-less practical jokes to play on the unsuspecting crew, they were playing video games.

One night, Corey Feldman figured out how to get the score on the video machine higher than it could ac-tually go. Worried about being found out, River, who was the oldest, said he'd take the blame if anything hap-pened.

Thinking back, he admits, "The motel managers weren't exactly thrilled with us." The young stars were often spotted at the motel's swimming pool when they weren't filming the movie. One morning, it was discov-ered that the pool had mysteriously drained itself the night before. Although the motel managers had a feeling the boys were responsible, they couldn't prove it. To this day, no one has ever found out what really happened.

All Wil says is, "We had most of our parties in the pool. We would take chairs and tables and throw them into the pool. Then we'd just sit there on the bottom."

The boys would spend hours laughing and talking, and River found he had a lot in common with Wil, Corey, and Jerry. "I think that the thing I'll remember most about *Stand By Me* is the friendships I made," he notes. "We all really got close. Of course, we argued over little things like who was going to walk down the railroad tracks first. But I think we'll always be friends, just like our characters were in the movie."

Stand By Me began production on June 17, 1985, and the first three weeks of filming were the most fun for River. He had really been looking forward to spending his summer in Oregon, the state he was born in. His family traveled with him to the movie location so they'd be able to spend time with River on the days he wouldn't be working.

The crew utilized a number of scenic and small-town sites within the state of Oregon. With very few changes, the historic town of Brownsville was transformed into the fictional Castle Rock, hometown for Chris and the other boys.

River plunged into his role wholeheartedly. When he arrived on the set that sunny June day, the first thing Rob Reiner gave his young cast was a cassette tape of the music that was going to be used in the film. Because the movie is set in 1960, before any of the young stars were even born, it was the only way Reiner felt they would be able to get acquainted with that time.

"We listened to the music over and over," recalls River,

who learned the words to the title tune and would wake up in the middle of the night singing it. "We even learned all the slang language they used back then," he adds.

Even at age fourteen, River carefully prepared for his role, meticulously studying his lines. "When I first start working on a role, I really go overboard," he asserts. "For about a week, I guess you could say I overact. Then for about three days, I just think about my lines . . . every single word. Once I start filming, I let everything go and just try to be as natural as possible."

The crew was able to capture the look and feel of small-town life in 1960 by filming in Oregon. There, they had the freedom to change store windows and drive in old Chevys for authenticity. Everything was perfect —the clothes, the music, the setting—and River felt proud to be part of it. Looking back on the fun-filled days he spent filming *Stand By Me,* River says with a twinkle in his eye, "That was, without a doubt, the best summer of my life."

The rest of the cast and crew also enjoyed the unusually hot and rainless Oregon summer. The filming took a total of sixty days. The company moved to the rugged Mount Shasta area of California for an additional two weeks to shoot the agonizing railroad track bridge scene.

During their odyssey, the boys are tempted to test fate by taking a dangerous shortcut over a ninety-foot-high wooden trestle. While slowly walking the track, a powerful locomotive engine turns the bend and the boys must run to their safety.

Reiner used safety lines when shooting the close-ups and stunt doubles for the long shots. The actual shot of the boys jumping off the track was filmed later on a Hollywood sound stage, but the four daring stars actually did run along the tracks. Later, Wil and River would admit their fear during the filming of this suspenseful scene. But they also admitted that the tense moment was necessary to add adventure to the film.

When the movie was released in August 1986, critics praised River's excellent performance of Chris Chambers, the troubled teenager. *The Hollywood Reporter,* a well-respected trade entertainment magazine, described him as "particularly outstanding." Interviewers said of him: "He has that weathered look of a solitary rider." "Independent." "Resilient." "Reliant." "Qualities of spirit that glue your eyes to the screen when you watch him."

But it wasn't only the critics who raved about River. Rob Reiner said in an interview that his favorite moment in the film is the campfire scene where River's character tearfully tells his side of the story after being accused of theft.

"For my money, it's the strongest scene in the entire film," he said. "I've seen the movie a thousand times and every time I see that scene, I cry. River was excellent in it."

Despite all the praise River was receiving, he modestly announced that he *didn't* like his performance in *Stand By Me*. "It's a great film," he said. "And people seemed to like my performance in it, but I didn't. Don't get me wrong, I'm really proud that I was in it, but I wanted to just sit back and enjoy it without having to see myself up there on the screen."

It's only been in the past year that River has begun to enjoy watching himself in *Stand By Me*, saying in a recent interview, "I have a tendency to be supercritical of myself. I just saw *Stand By Me* again and at least I was finally able to see it without cringing."

By the summer of 1986, River Phoenix was a full-fledged star. His name was fast becoming a household word and fans began writing to their favorite teen magazines asking questions about River, his life, and his career. With such an overwhelming response to this hot new star, magazines began putting small pictures of him on their covers.

"We had no idea *Stand By Me* was going to be so big and there were going to be all these eleven- and twelve-year-olds who'd be looking up to Riv," says his mom, Arlyn.

In a few months, River would receive hundreds of fan letters and gifts, which keep increasing as his popularity grows. His brother, Leaf, says, "River gets a lot of gifts, especially from Japan. They send him portraits, stuffed animals. He even got a watch from Sweden but he sent it back."

River couldn't believe the attention he was getting in such a short time. "He received intricate needlepoint pictures of himself," says Arlyn. "Some of his fans have sent money and we're always sending it back. River feels so bad about it."

His fans have always meant a lot to him. That's why he wants them to know that he's the same unspoiled guy he was before success came his way. "After *Stand By Me* came out people were telling me, 'You're so good,' 'You're going to be a star,' and things like that," he remembers. "You can't think about it. If you take it the wrong way, you can get really high on yourself. People get so lost when that happens to them. They may think they have everything under control, but everything is really out of control. Their lives are totally in pieces," adds this level-headed young man.

As a hot new Hollywood talent, every film producer in town soon wanted to sign River for his next picture. Offers began pouring into his agent's office and River used careful judgment in deciding what his next move would be. He knew the pitfalls of the business and was warned by people like Rob Reiner, who told him to be careful when choosing roles. Concerned with only doing quality movies, River didn't want to accept the wrong film as his next project.

This dedicated actor likes playing meaningful characters instead of appearing in mindless teenage films that glorify sex, violence, and drugs. "Those types of movies are distorted," he reveals. "The portrayal isn't real. The main problem is that they don't show how it really is to be a teenager today. They just try to make drugs and violence look cool and think that's right," he explains, shaking his head in disbelief.

After *Stand By Me,* River won a small role in a television movie that was just too exciting to turn down. The two-hour drama was called *Circle of Violence: A Family Drama,* and starred veteran actresses Geraldine Fitzgerald and Tuesday Weld. It was a heart-wrenching story which focused on the physical and mental abuse of a woman (Geraldine Fitzgerald) by her daughter (Tuesday Weld).

As Chris Benfield, the tormented child caught in the middle, River turned in a compelling performance. He enjoyed working on television again, even though it would be the last time he would appear on the small screen.

No sooner did he finish filming *Circle of Violence: A Family Drama* than he immediately started working on another feature film, *The Mosquito Coast*. It had been interesting to River that his first big break, *Stand By Me*, was shot in Oregon, where he was born.

But it was even more intriguing when he found out that *The Mosquito Coast* was to begin production in the Central American country Belize, near where River had spent part of his childhood.

7

FROM COAST TO COAST

For four months in 1986, River Phoenix found himself back in the raw jungle of Central America. Even though he was there to film his next movie, the setting brought back painful memories of his childhood. However, his recollections of the years he spent living in a foreign country helped him prepare for his role in *The Mosquito Coast*.

When River first read the script of this action-packed movie, he was amazed that his character's unusual life paralleled his own adventurous early years. A contemporary *Swiss Family Robinson* story, *The Mosquito Coast* is an exhilarating tale of how a family's quest for paradise and a simpler, more peaceful life becomes a terrifying fight for survival. River was cast in the role of Charlie Fox, the beleaguered oldest son, through whose eyes the story is told. That meant that River would not only be one of the movie's stars, he would also be narrating it. This film would prove to be one of the most exciting projects River would undertake as an actor.

River felt an immediate connection with his character. "I knew my character so well because I *was* that character," he declares. "I knew his whole past!"

Besides identifying with his role, River developed a close relationship with the film's star, Harrison Ford, who played his father, the fiercely independent Allie Fox. Possessed by a dream and fed up with society, Allie, an inventor, wants to escape with his family to a pure, untainted world. Packing up his wife (Helen Mirren), two sons (River and Jadrien Steele), and twin daughters (Hilary and Rebecca Gordon), he boards a freighter for the Mosquito Coast.

The film was based on Paul Theroux's 1982 best-selling novel of the same name. The author explains why he set his main characters in the subtropical jungle. While writing his immensely popular travel book *The Old Patagonia Express,* Theroux researched the Mosquito Coast and found it extraordinary. "The Mosquito Coast, which extends from Puerto Barrios in Guatemala to Colon in Panama, is wild and looks the perfect setting for the story of castaways," he wrote.

The task for director Peter Weir was to find the right location for the movie. It was interesting that of all the locations he scouted, he decided on Belize. "We had surveyed Jamaica, Costa Rica, Guatemala, Mexico, and Hawaii for the film," he says. "But Belize seemed to stand out. We found every location we needed there— mountains, ocean, jungle, rivers—all within one hour of Belize City."

In the film, the moment the Fox family leaves America to settle in the quiet of the jungle and ultimately embark on a new life, they experience a series of joys and tragedies. During the first half hour of the movie, Allie Fox purchases an abandoned "town" named Jeronimo, which is actually no more than a few shacks in an overgrown jungle clearing. At Jeronimo, the family builds a comfortable settlement complete with a kitchen, bedrooms, showers, and a garden. At the same time, Allie invents an ice machine that brings not only ice, but air conditioning to the town. For the family, it is the Garden of Eden until it is destroyed and they are forced to flee.

From the beginning, River felt a connection to the story. It seemed to hit home because of the experiences he endured as a child. He couldn't help remembering the time he and his family lived in a hut in Venezuela. During the production, River told one reporter, "This is kind of strange filming this movie right here. It's so close to where I spent a good part of my own childhood." He went on to explain that, although he was now living in the United States, he still felt different from other kids his age. "In many ways, I'm like a foreigner because I've lived differently from other teenagers," he openly admitted.

Given the similarities between River and his on-screen character, he seemed the perfect choice to portray Charlie Fox. But, oddly enough, he almost didn't win the role. Director Peter Weir, who directed *Gallipoli* and *The Year of Living Dangerously,* which made a star out of an unknown Mel Gibson, originally wanted a twelve- or thirteen-year-old for the crucial part of the oldest son. Fifteen-year-old River auditioned, but was immediately overlooked because of his age.

Weir continued to interview scores of younger actors.

At the same time, Diane Crittenden, the casting director, replayed some of the audition tapes and came across River's. His performance was riveting. She was so convinced he was the right actor for the role that she burst through Weir's door to tell him.

"There's a boy on this tape named River Phoenix," she said, handing the director a videocassette. "He's terrific, only he's fifteen."

Weir played River's test and was impressed. Still, he felt the actor was too old for the part and began auditioning other boys. When the director found himself unable to stop looking at River's audition tape, he read over the young actor's résumé. He couldn't believe River, like Charlie, spent part of his childhood traveling in Central and South America with his family. "I finally said to myself, 'What does it matter how old he is?'" recalls Weir. "He looks like Harrison's son. And I cast him!"

As one of the film's stars, River was in good company. He was thrilled to work with Harrison Ford, the star of the blockbusters *Star Wars, Raiders of the Lost Ark,* and *Witness* (also directed by Peter Weir), because he had admired him for so long. "Harrison is very courageous," says River, who admits he learned a lot about acting from Ford. "I think his performance in the movie shocked a lot of people."

As he ponders the chemistry he and Ford had as father and son in the film, River explains, "I didn't make him feel like he was some kind of superstar and I think he liked that. Sometimes Harrison would say a line with more intensity and my reaction would be different. We really played off each other well."

From the beginning, Harrison took River under his wing because he recognized three things in the enthusiastic young actor—intensity, talent, and a little of himself at River's age. "He is a natural actor," praises Ford. "He's inventive, smart, and susceptible to all kinds of influences. He is also very serious about his work."

Most of River's scenes are with Ford and, watching them together, it almost seems like they really are father and son going through a crisis. River feels the heart of *The Mosquito Coast* is its strong message. "The movie tells you to be true to the one you love," he explains.

It was something he found easy to relate to. Despite the problems the fictional Fox family had, they remained a close-knit group. It was not unlike River's own family, which had gone through similar occurrences, but always found strength as a family.

Off-screen, River's father accompanied him to Belize and stayed the entire four months. It was hard, in the beginning, for John to readjust to the harsh conditions of the jungle since he had grown accustomed to his life in California. "A common sight on the set of the film were large snakes, like boa constrictors, and alligators," recalls River's dad.

Most of the cast and crew lived in the jungle, with the exception of Harrison Ford, who stayed at the Belizian Hotel a few miles away. River learned to quickly adapt. "It was very hot," he begins. "And there were a lot of mosquitos, but I got used to it. We ate a lot of rice, mangoes, and coconuts, which is what I eat anyway."

Nearly everyone on the set had his share of bruises, cuts, mosquito bites, and heavy sunburn—minor problems they all learned to overlook. As Helen Mirren, who played River's mother in the film, said, "To actually experience the heat, the bugs, the mud, and the rain was a million times better than playing it on a studio back lot with a few palm trees."

The one problem the cast did have trouble adjusting to was the cultural isolation of Belize. There was absolutely no means of entertainment for miles around. To deal with this, several things were brought over from the States: two dozen VCRs with a vast selection of tapes, elaborate stereo systems, four computers, and a cappuccino machine. Bagels were even flown in from Miami.

Soon River and the rest of the cast and crew had all the comforts of home, and filming, for the most part, went smoothly. River worked all week and was tutored his usual three hours a day, along with the film's other young stars, Jadrien Steele and Martha Plimpton. It didn't take River long to become friends with Jadrien, but his early relationship with Martha had a rocky start.

The strong-minded actress comes from a show-business background; her father is veteran actor Keith Carradine, and her mother is stage actress Shelley Plimpton. In *The Mosquito Coast,* Martha played the reverend's daughter, Emily Spellgood, who is attracted to Charlie (River). Although the young stars would eventually become close off-screen and even work together again in the film *Running On Empty,* they literally hated each other when they first met. It was only after filming on *The Mosquito Coast* began that River noted, "We grew up and realized we had both changed a lot."

Halfway through production, while River was getting closer to Martha, he was surprised by pals Dweezil and Moon Unit Zappa, who flew to Belize for a visit. The three friends, all born under the sign of Virgo, had met at a party and found out they had similar likes and

At age ten, an adorable, boyish River starred on the TV series *Seven Brides for Seven Brothers*.
PHOTO BY DIANNA WHITLEY/SHOOTING STAR/PHOTO TRENDS

EXPLORERS

In *Explorers*, River (center) played a brainy, scientific kid named Wolfgang Muller. Ethan Hawke (left) and Jason Presson (right) co-starred in this tale of three boys who build a spaceship and take it into space.

COURTESY OF THE MEMORY SHOP

The *Stand By Me* boys. Left to right, Wil Wheaton, Corey Feldman, River, and Jerry O'Connell.
PHOTO TRENDS

WIL   **COREY**   **RIVER**   **JERRY**

STAND

River with Kiefer Sutherland in a tense scene from *Stand By Me*.
PHOTO TRENDS

BY ME

River and his *Stand By Me* co-star
and friend, Wil Wheaton.
PHOTO BY STEPHEN ELLISON/SHOOTING STAR/PHOTO TRENDS

River (second from left) with Harrison Ford in *The Mosquito Coast*. The film remains River's favorite screen role to date.
PICTORIAL PARADE

THE MOSQUITO COAST

SUMMER

LIBERTY

LEAF

RIVER

RAINBOW

A Phoenix pyramid: River and Rainbow (bottom), Liberty and Leaf (middle) and Summer (top).
PHOTO BY STEPHEN ELLISON/SHOOTING STAR/PHOTO TRENDS

The talented Phoenix family. Left to right, Rainbow, River, Liberty, Summer, Leaf, and parents, John and Arlyn.

PHOTO BY STEPHEN ELLISON/SHOOTING STAR/PHOTO TRENDS

No flashy clothes for this superstar. River is most comfortable wearing jeans and a T-shirt.

PHOTO BY STEPHEN ELLISON/
SHOOTING STAR/PHOTO TRENDS

Surrounded by the crew of *Little Nikita*, River gets ready to film his scene.
PHOTO BY VINNIE ZUFFANTE/STAR FILE

LITTLE NIKITA

Sidney Poitier, who starred opposite River in *Little Nikita*, says, "I feel River Phoenix is one of our finest young actors and destined to leave an indelible imprint on American film."
PHOTO BY VINNIE ZUFFANTE/STAR FILE

Serious-minded River takes a break during the filming of *Little Nikita*.
PHOTO BY VINNIE ZUFFANTE/STAR FILE

Here's River, looking as handsome
as ever.
PHOTO BY STEPHEN ELLISON/SHOOTING STAR/PHOTO TRENDS

The number one teen movie star today.

PHOTO BY STEPHEN ELLISON/SHOOTING STAR/PHOTO TRENDS

"I want to get more involved in music," confides River, who writes his own songs and plays guitar, bass, and piano.
PHOTO BY STEPHEN ELLISON/SHOOTING STAR/PHOTO TRENDS

River's flying high whenever he starts strumming his guitar.
PHOTO BY STEPHEN ELLISON/SHOOTING STAR/PHOTO TRENDS

Thinking ahead to his future, River says, "I want to play every character — but only once. I like to experience things."
PHOTO BY STEPHEN ELLISON/SHOOTING STAR/PHOTO TRENDS

dislikes. "Whenever I'm with Dweezil and Moon, we have a blast," notes River. "When we hang out together and are introduced to people who don't know our names, it's something to watch their reactions," he adds, laughing.

River couldn't believe Dweezil and Moon flew all the way to Central America just to see him. He spent a few days between filming catching up with the children of rock star Frank Zappa before they headed back to California.

On the weekends, River found himself involved in a host of activities during breaks from shooting the movie. He and his father loved snorkeling in the barrier reef coastline, and sometimes River and Jadrien went searching the jungle for jaguars.

River was also spotted talking to the people of Belize. He found working with them to be a great experience because their culture was so different from his own. Three hundred Belizians were hired to work on *The Mosquito Coast*. It was soon apparent that the movie was the biggest thing ever to hit the town, and the Belizians talked about it from the moment the movie company arrived to the time they left.

They were fascinated with the filming, and many of the local residents quizzed River about the movie, his role in it, and how he felt about being an actor. River graciously took the opportunity to talk to them because he was just as interested in their lifestyle as they were in his.

Over the next four months, on the set of *The Mosquito Coast,* River Phoenix underwent a change in his physical appearance. When filming began, he was just five feet five and still slightly on the chubby side. By the end of production, all his baby fat was gone. He had grown a full three inches in height and lost twenty pounds.

River has fond memories of *The Mosquito Coast,* and it remains his personal favorite of all his films. Maybe it was because he was able to relate so closely to the story and his character. To River, it was an emotional film that combined many sad and funny moments. "I did my best work in *The Mosquito Coast,*" he divulges. "I know it wasn't such a big hit, but for me it was more meaningful than anything else I'd ever done."

As always, River received critical plaudits for his performance and he knew he had made the right move by accepting a supporting role in *The Mosquito Coast.* By costarring in the film opposite an established actor like Harrison Ford, River had proved he was more than just another teen star—he was a serious-minded actor. As his agent, Iris Burton, says, "River is a strong, intense young actor with great longevity."

In just one year, River Phoenix had become a hot young star to look out for. He had completed three successful movies in less than two years and everyone in Hollywood was buzzing about him. Major magazines and television talk shows wanted to interview him. River obliged for the sake of his movies, but he has never really liked opening up and talking about himself.

Agreeing to grant journalists interviews, River talked about his early life, but focused more on his career. Interviewers liked talking to him because they never knew what to expect. He once granted a journalist an interview while hanging upside down on an exercise bar. Other times, his entire family was present, drinking in every word spoken by River and the journalist.

With *The Mosquito Coast* completed, River and his father

returned home to the California coast. The Phoenix family still hadn't found a big enough home. But all this would soon change. Almost immediately after River and his dad returned to California, the family moved into a twenty-acre ranch in San Diego.

The move happened at a good point in River's life. He liked the free feeling of going outdoors and being close to nature. Though many thought he would take a much-deserved rest after filming three movies back to back, he wasn't about to slow down. This was only the beginning and he was eager to get back in front of the cameras.

Without reaping the rewards of his newfound fame, River began searching for his next project. He is the kind of actor who grows impatient between assignments. Once he finishes a movie, he likes to know he has something else lined up to begin working on right away.

By this time, *Stand By Me* had become the sleeper hit of the year, and the next project River agreed to appear in was the video of the title song. Ben E. King, who had had a number one hit with the tune back in 1961, rerecorded it for the movie and it climbed the charts again. The only cast members of the film to appear in the video were River and Wil Wheaton. When they took time to chat with *Entertainment Tonight,* the popular entertainment show, both boys admitted that filming the video was a little bit tense, but a lot of fun.

After appearing in three dramatic movies, River Phoenix decided to break from his tradition and accepted the title role in a comedy called *Jimmy Reardon* (later changed to *A Night in the Life of Jimmy Reardon*). The film had its problems right from the beginning—

one of the biggest being its R rating and the fact that many of River's teenage fans couldn't get in to see it.

His parents had warned him not to take the role in the teen sex comedy, but he didn't listen. He was looking for a new challenge and thought it would be a good experience. It was only afterward that River thought maybe his parents had been right.

A Night in the Life of Jimmy Reardon was the first River Phoenix movie to receive mixed reviews.

8

RIVER PHOENIX VS. JIMMY REARDON

If nothing else came out of River's Jimmy Reardon experience, he at least realized he never wants to *be* like his character. "Jimmy is about as far from the real me as you can get," he asserts. "He is more manipulative and bolder with women."

Jimmy Reardon can be considered River's first adult role. He was just sixteen years old when he plunged into the life of eighteen-year-old Jimmy. "I wanted to play an older character and decided to go for it," says River enthusiastically. "Overall, it was a great experience even though I can see how I would probably have more insight playing a young character when I'm older."

The movie marked a few firsts for River. "This is the first time in which I've done any kind of love scenes and it's also my first comedy. I felt almost guilty getting paid!" he pronounces with a mischievous grin.

Although River would play his first comedic role with success, he admits he was a little uneasy in the beginning. "I think that comedy can be really boring, especially if you copy from someone else," he says. "That's why I don't watch television!"

A Night in the Life of Jimmy Reardon received an R rating from the board of censors, demanding that some of River's more revealing love scenes be cut. What remained still startled River's fans and parents.

When John and Arlyn first saw their son on-screen, they were shocked. "It was hard for my father to see that it wasn't really me," explains the young superstar.

He insists that *Jimmy Reardon,* like all his movies, has a very important message. As an actor, River is constantly concerned with expressing himself on-screen in a way that will reach out to people who see his movies, and maybe even help them in their own lives. *Stand By Me*'s positive theme centered on friendship, and *The Mosquito Coast*'s message was love. The message in *A Night in the Life of Jimmy Reardon,* according to River, is "to slow down and think about what you're doing before you do it. You've got to weigh the pros and cons and go with what's best for you. Of course, you can get paranoid analyzing each situation you're faced with. Sometimes, you've got to go with your instincts."

That is exactly what River did when he first decided to take the lead role as the irrepressible Jimmy Reardon, seeing it as a departure for him both personally and professionally. To prepare for his role, River once again thought about his character's existence beyond the script. "I created an outline of his whole past so his actions would be understandable," he explained.

The rambunctious comedy was based on the 1967 novel *Aren't You Ever Gonna Kiss Me Goodbye?* by William Reichert, who also wrote and directed the movie. Set in

1962, the film covers thirty-six hours in the life of the main character, the romantic poet Jimmy Reardon. As in *The Mosquito Coast,* River is the narrator of the film as well as the star. It is told by Jimmy himself, looking back on the turning points in his adolescent life.

On the threshold of adulthood, Jimmy is prepared for anything life has to offer, but he is still too young to make adult decisions. His family has recently moved to Evanston, Illinois, a ritzy suburb of Chicago, and it doesn't take Jimmy long to become acquainted with the rich kids in town. Among them are Lisa (Meredith Salenger), who desires Jimmy but doesn't trust him; Fred (Matthew L. Perry), who becomes Jimmy's loyal but naive best friend; Suzie (Louanne), the know-it-all of the group; and Denise (Ione Skye), who is Fred's girlfriend, but spends Saturday afternoons in Jimmy's arms.

While his friends are all getting ready to go to Ivy League universities, Jimmy's dad (Paul Koslo) demands that he go to his alma mater, the dull McKinley business college. Seeing his life as a repeat of his father's, Jimmy panics and rebels. He becomes involved with neighbor Joyce Fickett (Ann Magnuson), a divorcée who has had her eye on the young Casanova.

Over the next day and a half, Jimmy must come face-to-face with his future and ultimately come to terms with growing up. Eventually, he sees his friends and parents in a different light and realizes that he and his father have more in common than they ever dreamed possible.

"It's not a stereotypical 'coming-of-age' film," explains River. "Because it's all seen through Jimmy's poetic point of view, and it doesn't really have a happy ending—nor should it. He took a wrong turn somewhere along the line. Still, we care about him because we know his intentions are beautiful. He wants to go to Hawaii with Lisa, the girl of his dreams, and live in paradise. Everybody wants that.

"Jimmy gets carried away by all his dreams, which he wants to make happen in a day and a half," adds River, further discussing his role. "My own life has been changed dramatically over the course of a day and a half, so what happens to Jimmy is very believable to me."

River's fellow costars all looked up to him on the set. Meredith Salenger (*The Journey of Natty Gann*) happily delineates the virtues of her gorgeous leading man and says, "River is down-to-earth and really special."

Matthew L. Perry, who originally auditioned for the role of Jimmy Reardon and was cast as Fred, says of River, "Working with him has been great because I had seen *Stand By Me* and thought he was wonderful in it. He really helped me through some of my scenes.

"I remember the first day of shooting," Matthew continues. "It was seven-fifteen in the morning and I had the first line. So, there I was sitting next to River, who was all ready to go, and I was nervous and shaking. Whenever I messed up a line throughout the production, he'd say, 'Look, if you make a mistake, don't worry. We'll get it right. We have all day.' "

A Night in the Life of Jimmy Reardon was filmed entirely on location in and around Chicago, Illinois. When River left for the Windy City, his grandfather went with him. One member of the Phoenix family always accompanies River on the sets of his movies. "I've been on the road a lot with Riv," says his mom. "We try to be there for him."

Arlyn didn't want to inhibit her son during the filming of *Jimmy Reardon* and thought it was a good idea for his grandfather to watch over him this time. Once they arrived in Chicago, River's routine was simple. As soon as filming was over for the day, he would go back to his hotel room, read his script, and go to sleep.

Says Matthew Perry, "That's where we were different. I *lived* Chicago. I went everywhere and did everything while I was there."

When the film wrapped and River returned home, Arlyn immediately saw a change in him. "He grew up during that film," she comments. "Not just as an actor, but also as a young man. I had seen a difference in him from one movie to the next because he changes like a chameleon with each role he plays. But it was more apparent after *Jimmy Reardon*. He even decided to wear his hair a little longer and he likes to keep it in his face."

Though River basically had a good time filming *A Night in the Life of Jimmy Reardon,* it received mixed reviews from critics. River's performance, however, did not go unnoticed, nor did his talented young costars.

Wrote *Elle* magazine, "River Phoenix, the 'hot-throb' from *Stand By Me,* is right at home in this film's universe of terrific young talent." *The Hollywood Reporter* singled out River and wrote, "River Phoenix deserves credit for making something of his cocky, chip-on-the-shoulder part; at times, he bounds around like a well-scrubbed Cagney, fitting his wrong-side-of-the-track nature."

River wasn't completely disappointed with the reaction people had toward his first comedic venture. He had enjoyed being part of it; he even wrote the film's theme song, which was exciting.

It made him realize that music was still important to him and, once again, he dreamed of becoming a musician. This time, however, his dream was about to become a reality.

9

PRIVATE TIME

There are so many different sides of River Phoenix, yet no one knows what he's really like in private. His fans have seen their favorite guy in a variety of roles on the silver screen; from a caring teenager in *Stand By Me* and *The Mosquito Coast* to a junior-league Don Juan in *A Night in the Life of Jimmy Reardon*. But who is the *real* River Phoenix? What is he like off-screen? Of all the different characters he's played, which one is closest to his own personality?

"I guess you could say I'm most like the character I'm playing at the moment," he reveals. "When I decide to play a part, I jump into it and *become* the person I'm playing."

It appears to some that River constantly works and churns out one movie after another. But he doesn't spend *all* his time acting. He has a long list of things that he enjoys doing when the cameras stop rolling.

For one thing, music is a very important part of River's life. He finds it relaxing to shut himself in his bedroom and practice his guitar. River is a very gifted songwriter and has penned dozens of his own tunes. He sings, arranges, and records all his songs on his four-track tape recorder. What began as a hobby for River may very well become a second career for this multitalented young man.

Still dreaming of a career in music, he got the bright idea to send one of his demo tapes to Island Records, an affiliate of Island Pictures, which distributed *A Night in the Life of Jimmy Reardon*. They had been impressed with River's musical talents since first hearing the song he wrote for the movie, and it didn't take them long to sign him to a recording contract.

It's the opportunity River has been waiting for, and he is very excited about crossing over into music. After so many years of wanting a music career, the people closest to River expected him to begin working on his debut album immediately. But River claims he's in no hurry to rush a record out.

"There are so many actors who have come out with albums these days," he says. "I don't want to do it just because it's the thing to do."

The folks at Island Records aren't worried. They are willing to wait until River is ready. "We think he will be around for a long time," smiles Kim Buie of Island Records. "So there's no need to rush him."

Right now, River is putting together a package of the songs he wants to include on the album. One song he is writing will utilize the musical talents of the rest of the Phoenix kids. "We all sing," says River proudly. "Whenever we are all together, we take our instruments out and play. Rainbow and I do vocals. I play guitar, bass, and piano. My brother, Leaf, plays drums, and Liberty and Summer sing background vocals. It's a lot of fun. It's like we're our own rock band," he adds.

As a movie idol, top teen heartthrob, and sex symbol to millions of adoring fans, River remains modest and down-to-earth about his skyrocketing success. Despite his fame and fortune, he hasn't gone Hollywood—and probably never will! River doesn't like the party scene nor the glamour and glitz of Hollywood. He'd much rather stay home and spend time with his family and close friends.

Friends are very important to River. Some of his best pals are Dweezil and Moon Unit Zappa and his *Stand By Me* costar Wil Wheaton. "Honesty means a lot to me," he says. "If you want to be my friend, you have to be honest with me. I can identify with people like Dweezil, Moon, and Wil. We have some things in common and we get along great. I don't have a lot of time to be with my friends because of my busy schedule, so the time I do have is precious."

Even though family and friends are important to him, there are times when he enjoys quiet moments by himself. "I do need to be alone and unwind once in a while," he says. "But I never want to be totally alone. I like to know that I have a loving family and friends that really care about me when I need them."

On the occasions when he is by himself, he often goes into his room and reads some of his fan mail. River feels great when people write to him and he tries to answer as much of the mail as he can. "The most rewarding thing about being an actor is when people send me letters and tell me they've been affected by my work," he offers. "When they say things like they really identified with a character I played and that it really helped them, it's a great feeling. It's so nice that I can touch so many people and be a friend through my movies."

When River received a letter from an ill fan, he went out of his way to offer him comfort. The young boy was in the hospital when he saw a videocassette of *Stand By Me*. He saw River as someone who could be his friend and decided to write to him.

In just two weeks, River called his young fan and spoke to him for over an hour on the telephone. "River gave me a new outlook on life," said the boy. "He cared enough to give me something I never had—a friend."

As an actor in the public eye, River Phoenix is in the unique position of reaching out to people in need, and he tries to help others as much as possible. While many things bring a smile to River's face—like acting, his music, and spending time with his family—this sensitive young man admits that he is sad when he thinks about wars and world problems. He is concerned with making films that will be educational to other kids. "Some people think I'm a softy," explains River. "But I'm offended by the way people treat each other sometimes."

He gets very upset about the plight of the homeless and has publicly stated that one day he hopes to open a shelter for homeless children. Another of River's secret wishes is to live in a peaceful world where pain does not exist.

There is no limit to River Phoenix's dreams. He is confident, independent, and marches to the beat of his own drum. He doesn't concern himself with what other people say about him. River likes to do things his own way.

How does this strong, healthy, handsome actor keep

in such great shape? At five feet ten and a half inches and 155 pounds, River drinks a lot of orange juice and eats mostly vegetables and fresh fruits. His favorite foods are vegetarian dishes, Chinese meals, tofu (which is a high-protein food), and fresh fruits like peaches, plums, apples, mangoes, coconuts, and melons.

Besides eating plenty of the right foods, River also finds time for exercise. He is very athletic, and when he has free time, he loves going to the beach, where he soaks in the golden sunshine. His favorite sports include swimming, surfing, bicycling, rock climbing, and playing football and basketball with his siblings.

When it comes to clothes, River doesn't like to wear anything trendy or flashy. He dresses more for comfort than for fashion and often sports a T-shirt and jeans. He wears a size-nine shoe and gets the most use out of worn-out sneakers. Because his favorite colors are blue and black, you will most likely find this stunner dressed in darker colors.

"I like some brighter colors," he confides. "But black or blue are so much nicer because the darkness makes you more radiant."

Month after month River's face lights up the covers of major teen magazines, but fans very rarely see him smile in the countless photos. While other teen idols continually smile for the cameras, River has decided to maintain a different kind of image.

In one of his latest photo sessions, three photographers tried for eight hours to crack him up, but had no luck. "We told every kind of joke in the book," said one of the photographers. "He just kept telling us he wanted to look serious."

With more and more photos featuring a thoughtful

River Phoenix, the question was bound to be asked. In a recent interview, one reporter asked River why he chooses not to smile. He was happy to explain his reason.

"It's real important to me that people don't get the wrong impression," he said. "And that's why I'm careful about how I look when I have to have my picture taken. I don't want to look like, you know, Mr. G.Q. I want to look like me. I don't want to pose with a full-on, wonderful smile because that looks posed or phony. I don't want to put an obnoxious image in someone's mind. I'd rather have people see me as real and natural and friendly," he concluded.

River comes across as an ideal young man, someone who is handsome, caring, impressionable, charming. Like any other eighteen-year-old, he thinks about girls and about meeting the right girl for him. His only romantic conflict now is that he's so busy he feels it wouldn't be fair to ask one girl to be faithful to him.

"A relationship means fifty-fifty as far as I'm concerned," River states. "How can I expect that from a girl when my fifty percent is being taken up with filming movies and traveling. It's hard right now to date anyone steady because I'm always on the go."

River has a definite idea of the kind of girl he is attracted to. First of all, girls who expect special treatment from him are a total turn-off. "If I don't like someone's attitude, I won't hang around with them," he says. "That goes for girls, too. If I meet a girl who is really snobby and wants special treatment, she's not going to get it from me because she hasn't earned it. But I haven't really been bothered by anyone like that. Most of the girls I've met have been real nice—and that's what attracts me!"

River likes girls who take pride in their appearance, but are also very natural. He doesn't like someone who wears too much makeup or fusses with hair or clothes. "I'm a natural actor," he professes. "And I'm natural in everything I do. The girl I go out with should be the same."

It is also important to River that his girlfriend be independent and able to talk to him about everything. "I need to feel that I can share my feelings," he says. "I like a girl who is fun to be around and who I can talk to about real things—not just about the weather. I really like sharing thoughts."

River doesn't mind dating actresses because he feels they understand his busy schedule. He's gone out with Martha Plimpton on and off for two years. Some say the two stars are going steady; others say they're just good friends. River and Martha haven't commented, but they've been seen together on more than one or two occasions.

After meeting and striking up a close friendship on the set of *The Mosquito Coast,* they were cast as lovers in River's new movie *Running On Empty,* which was filmed on location in New York City. After filming for the day was through, River and Martha went out to eat in New York restaurants and became quite close. Only time will tell if Martha is the girl who will win River's heart.

Right now, he is devoting all his time to his career. In June 1988, he graduated high school, and he is now working full time as an actor. At just eighteen years old, River knows exactly what he wants out of life and is going after it full force. Ironically, while he hopes to educate teenagers through his movies, he has no immediate plans to continue his own education.

"I'd rather live than read about living," he assures. "I don't feel that I need college to prepare for life—I'm living it!"

River Phoenix is also living the life of one of the busiest and most successful young actors in Hollywood.

10

MEET THE
PHOENIX FAMILY

River isn't the only talented Phoenix in his family. Though he was John and Arlyn's first child to enter the world of show business, his younger siblings soon followed in their big brother's footsteps. It didn't take Rainbow, Leaf, and Summer long to nab roles on the big and small screens and to share the spotlight with their older brother. His sister Liberty also recently began an acting career of her own; she has appeared in two television commercials.

The Phoenixes are very supportive of each other; they feel their strength lies in the power of love they share as a family. They are so close that it's very rare to talk about one member of the family without including the rest of them. With all the hard times behind them, River and his loving clan are happy over all the success they've achieved in such a short time.

But, according to River, this success is no mere coincidence. He feels his family's faith and determination to overcome those bleak early years have helped everyone prosper. With all the creative juices that continually flow from the Phoenix family, River feels lucky to be part of such a positive group of people.

"I'm often asked if I'll always be part of this family," he says. "The answer is yes. I've got a good battery charge here. I go back home to my family to plug in. That's why I'll always want to spend a lot of time at Camp Phoenix."

River's and his siblings' careers are managed by their parents, who keep a close eye on their business affairs and make sure none of their little actors are getting too big for their britches. Regardless of the recognition they receive, there are no "stars" in the Phoenix household. As soon as River and his siblings come home after a day of filming, they are expected to do household chores. That means taking out the garbage, doing the laundry, and sometimes even preparing the vegetarian dishes for the family's dinners. River doesn't mind helping out and neither do his brother and sisters.

"We're all really close friends," says River's younger brother, Leaf. "We ride bikes a lot and all hang out together. Whenever there is a problem, we all sit down and talk about the situation. We try to fix whatever's wrong."

Unlike River, who dreamed of entering show business at an early age, Leaf never expected to become an actor. "I wanted to be a lot of different things," he expounds. "I like animals and I love to swim—swimming is my favorite sport—but I never thought much about what I wanted to be when I grew up."

It was after River landed his role on *Seven Brides for Seven Brothers* that Leaf decided acting was fun. After casting River, the producers decided they needed a younger child, also, and Leaf tried out for the role.

He didn't get it, but he did get the acting bug. He began auditioning and guest-starred on several television series, including *Hill Street Blues, Murder She Wrote* (where he and Summer played brother and sister), *The Fall Guy,* and *Morningstar, Eveningstar.* He also starred in the television pilots *Six Pack* and *Looking for Love* before making his feature-film debut in *Spacecamp,* followed by a lead role in *Russkies* (also costarring Summer as his on-screen sister, Candi).

Like River, husky-voiced Leaf Phoenix is a terrific young actor who has a bright future ahead of him. Dedicated to his craft, he convincingly portrays each role and looks up to his big brother as his role model. Without ever taking a real acting lesson, Leaf admits he learned everything he knows from his brother.

"River is amazing," he proclaims. "He's really a good actor. My favorite movie is *Stand By Me;* River was great in it. He plays all his parts so well. He actually changes even when he's off-camera; it's just instinct."

Leaf is astonished by the way River has handled his sudden surge of success. "He's not stuck-up at all," he notes. "I think he's handled his success really good. He's normal and friendly, just like he always was. And just like everybody else in my family is."

River's sister Rainbow is also acting full time and enjoying every minute of it. She has guest-starred on an episode of *Family Ties* as a singer in an all-girl band, and landed a juicy role in the Ally Sheedy movie *Maid To Order.* In that film, she played bratty Brie Starkey, a spoiled youngster who confronts heiress-turned-housekeeper Ally.

"It was a great experience because I got a chance to play a character so different from my own personality," she says. "In the film, I do terrible things to Ally, like stealing jewelry and blaming it on her. But in the end, my character changes for the better," she concludes.

Though some of Rainbow's meatier scenes ended up on the cutting room floor, she was very impressive in her first feature-film role.

Summer, the youngest Phoenix, has appeared twice with brother Leaf, in *Murder She Wrote* and *Russkies,* playing his on-screen sister. She also won a role as a friend of Ben Seaver's on the enormously popular TV series *Growing Pains,* and has appeared on the television show, *Airwolf,* a pilot for *Family Ties* called *All The Way Home* with Scott Valentine, and the TV movie *Kate's Secret* opposite Meredith Baxter-Birney.

Says Summer of her big brother, "I love River! He's such a talented actor that I go to him when I need help with my own acting. He gives me great advice. I really miss him when he's away from home."

Surprisingly, the Phoenixes decided to move from their Southern California ranch early last year. They are now spending time in Royal Palm Beach, Florida; their next step is buying a house in Venezuela or Mexico. They believe those countries are beautiful, and far from the traffic and confusion of big-city life.

"We all have a goal," states River. "We want to buy a new house and we're all working on it together. We like changes. It's important to our family to be together wherever we decide to settle."

The Phoenixes are strong-minded and motivated. Because of this, they will never fall into the trappings of Hollywood. They are grateful for the opportunities they've been given and remain, above all, a family of overachievers.

There is no sibling rivalry among the Phoenix kids; they enjoy lending one another support in their individual careers. Speaking about his family, River says, "In our house, it was never 'me'—always 'we.' And it still is like that. I think I would have loved them even if we weren't related. My family are real good people."

In just a short time, the Phoenix kids have accumulated quite an impressive list of credits. Many people have speculated that success is bound to change this family, but Arlyn is quick to disagree. "Show business won't spoil this family," she quips. "I really think there is a purpose why all this is happening to us. We just have to be patient and let that purpose find us."

There's no denying the fact that the Phoenixes are famous. Even though times are now easier for the tight-knit group, they haven't let success change them. On the contrary, they remain secure, positive, and ready for what the future holds. "The opportunities these kids have is amazing," says Arlyn. "The places they've traveled to and the people they've met have given them confidence.

"My husband John and I have been blessed with five extraordinary children," she continues with an engaging smile. "I look at them sometimes and wonder why they're mine." She pauses, thinks, and adds, almost hesitantly, "Maybe someday we can make a difference in the world."

Somehow, it seems like River and his family already have.

11

HOLLYWOOD HERO

"This is a great script! It's really good because I have so many confrontation scenes with different people. You see a lot of different levels and a lot of different personalities in Jeff. You see a gradual change from a carefree kid into a responsible person."

That was how River Phoenix summarized his character, Jeff Grant, in his next film, *Little Nikita*. He completely immersed himself in the role of a teenager whose world is turned upside down.

In the film, River plays an only child who finds himself torn between love for his country and love for his family. Veteran screen actor Sidney Poitier plays Roy Parmenter, an FBI agent who uncovers startling information that Jeff's parents are actually Russian spies. The secret leads the young man into international espionage and forces him to grow up overnight.

This movie is no light teen film. It required more than just a pretty face; the teenager who would play the critical role of Jeff Grant had to possess natural talent. With so many teenage actors in movies today, River Phoenix, who seemed to stand out far above the rest, undoubtedly received the most attention from critics and fellow actors. Everyone who has ever worked with him agrees that he is a very special young man.

While *A Night in the Life of Jimmy Reardon* was still in production, River was offered the part of Jeff in *Little Nikita*. He had garnered a solid reputation as an actor who plays characters of depth and emotional maturity, and people were taking notice of him. It seemed like his years of hard work and perseverance had paid off: River was now in a position to be even more selective in choosing his rules.

As he quickly adjusted to this new level of success, River read through the script for *Little Nikita*. He had made it clear that he would do no more comedies, at least for the time being. He got that out of his system with *Jimmy Reardon*. What he was looking for in his next screen role was another drama that he could sink his teeth into.

After reading the first few pages of *Little Nikita,* he knew he had found what he was looking for.

River's role required special contemplation. "It's shocking, depressing, and frustrating because Jeff can't really do anything about his past," he comments. "He's faced with hard decisions and must leave his teenage world and grow up."

In the beginning of *Little Nikita,* River's character seems to be a typical teen living in the small fictitious town of Fountain Grove, California, where he is taking part in the town's Armed Forces Day parade. "The opening looks like Norman Rockwell," says director Richard

Benjamin, who began his own career as an actor. "It's almost like, 'What's wrong with this picture?' It opens sunny and bright and then dramatically changes."

Benjamin says the energy between Poitier and rising star River Phoenix was dynamic. "River is a young actor who stayed right up with Poitier all the way," he says. "They have great chemistry. River has wonderful instincts. He is not only a superb actor, but he is real. He cannot fake; that's not in River, only the truth is in him, and it's wonderful to see. He has one foot in childhood and one foot in adulthood."

Benjamin had so much faith in his young star that he very rarely told River what to do on camera. Instead he let him "discover things by himself." Naturally, the director was pleased with the results. "I got things from River that I didn't even plan on because it came from inside him," said Benjamin during a recent interview.

The good relationship River and his director had was a tremendous help for the young actor. "Richard can relate to us," he says. "There was great communication. He always made things very clear. He's an easygoing person and it's really nice to work with a director like that. He'll be acting behind the camera, you know, and you can feel that energy and it helps," adds River, recalling the filming of *Little Nikita*.

The chemistry River and Sidney Poitier had on-screen was largely due to the fact that they also had a good off-screen relationship. River cherished the opportunity to work with the legendary Poitier and he learned a lot from him. "I learned not to take everything personally," he says. "Not to take the negative things about your acting personally and not to take this fame personally. It's just a job and I'm just trying to do it well.

Sidney's very consistent in his acting and in how he handles himself on and off the set. He's really spontaneous and real, and he has a reservoir to draw from that's amazing."

Poitier, who hadn't acted in almost ten years, returned to the screen in 1988 in *Shoot To Kill* and *Little Nikita*. He immediately found that acting opposite River was very challenging. "As an actor, River is so naturally gifted," he praises. "He is a very special kind of person. You're not working against an actor who's relying on technique. You're working against raw talent and that's very invigorating to me—he sparkles. River is so spontaneous and so quick, it charges my batteries."

The movie was shot mainly in and around San Diego, California, near the Phoenixes' ranch before they moved. The location for the film's fictitious town of Fountain Grove was actually shot in two California towns: La Mesa, outside of San Diego, and Monrovia, near Los Angeles. The movie's opening scene of the Armed Forces Day parade includes thousands of local residents along the streets. Among the crowd were many young people who turned out especially to catch a glimpse of River.

Even though he would stop and talk to fans during breaks, River didn't want reporters or photographers on the set. Why? The reason was simple. As an actor playing such a serious character, River needed to concentrate. He found it hard to step out of character and be himself. There would be plenty of time for interviews later on; but during filming, he was only concerned with doing the best job possible.

Most of River's more dramatic scenes were filmed in San Diego, near the San Diego Bay and along the picturesque coastline of Torrey Pines. Though River liked traveling to locations in San Diego he had never seen, he maintained a busy schedule of school and work that left very little time for leisure. Said one source on the set, "River would gear himself up for a really intense scene and once filming was over, he had to go and study a chapter of his social studies book or something."

But that didn't interfere with the spectacular performance he turned in. Halfway through production of *Little Nikita,* the unit publicist was quoted as saying, "River is absolutely wonderful in this film. I was watching some of the stuff he's done and I saw him in *Stand By Me* and *The Mosquito Coast* and he's progressed to a new level. This role takes River into a whole different form of acting than we've seen from him before."

By the time *Little Nikita* wrapped production, River already had another movie lined up. Filming three movies back to back may seem like grueling work, but River loved it and anxiously dove into his next project. Titled *Running On Empty,* this film took River on location to New York and New Jersey and reacquainted him with girlfriend Martha Plimpton, who won the role of Lorna, River's on-screen love interest. He was equally excited to be working with the well-respected director Sidney Lumet.

In *Running On Empty,* River plays Daniel Pope, a teen trying to free himself of his parents' past mistakes. He is the son of 1960's political activists Arthur and Annie Pope (played by Judd Hirsch of *Taxi* and Christine Lahti of *Housekeeping*), who are on the FBI's "Ten Most Wanted List" for bombing a government laboratory in the sixties. For the past twenty years they've been on the run from the law, living as fugitives and hiding out in different towns.

Danny, their older son, is a gifted pianist who wants to attend Juilliard. Unfortunately, he is caught in the middle of his parents' dilemma and can't pursue his dream without blowing their cover. Even though River had played an older character in *A Night in the Life of Jimmy Reardon,* his role as Danny could very well be the most important performance of his career.

Filming on the East Coast, in New York and New Jersey, meant packing up and moving to new surroundings for a while. This time, River's younger sister Summer wanted to join him in the Big Apple. As Summer recalls, "We all missed River like crazy, but I was the one who cried the hardest."

Though his parents also went with him, they allowed River his freedom. "He is seventeen now," said his mother in an interview at the time of production. "And he could be by himself. But you don't want to be alone in a city like New York, much less when you're seventeen."

River's dad, John, who is not only responsible for his oldest son's career but for his other children's as well, says with a grin, "The kids started growing so much that the most important thing I can do now is help them do whatever they want. I'm learning to butt out when I'm not needed." As far as River is concerned, he will always need his folks. He likes having them around and often goes to them for advice on his career. It helps him to see their point of view, even though River makes his own final decisions.

Near the end of filming on *Running On Empty,* as River was about to celebrate his eighteenth birthday, he sat back and thought of everything he had accomplished. He had achieved so much in such a short period of time. Still, he knows he has a long way to go in his career.

Perhaps the definitive image of River growing up is River Phoenix the dreamer: the little boy living in a hut in a faraway country, dreaming of becoming an actor. When his dream did come true, he worked hard at developing his natural talent. He loved the work right from the start and wanted to take it to higher levels. While other boys were outside playing, River was working.

He continues to push himself because he strives for perfection in all his roles. That's one of the reasons why he decided to play such diversified characters in his current three films. And, still, with all that he has experienced in his career, River admits, "I need time to broaden my mind."

He plans to travel to new, exotic places that he hasn't seen yet. He feels that by doing this he will experience firsthand other cultures and places. "I'd like to get to know the world a little better," he announces. "I think it would help me in developing and portraying my characters. I'd have more to draw from."

River Phoenix is candid when he speaks about his dreams and plans. With such a lustrous future ahead of him, it's hard to believe that River will ever make a wrong turn. He considers acting his job; he doesn't wallow in being a superstar. River Phoenix, the most popular teen hero and heartthrob today, is one of those rare types in show business.

While he is definitely an inspiration to young people through his meaningful films and positive outlook on life, he has a hard time describing himself. When he is asked this question, the first thing River says is, "That's tough."

As he scratches his head and thinks further about his own personality, this perplexed actor sums it up pretty well. "Let's see—I can't tell a joke, that's for sure, and I'm moody sometimes. But I think I'm a good guy!"

12

TOMORROW

In a January 17, 1988, article in *Newsday* titled "Their Stars Are Rising," River Phoenix was chosen as one of five newcomers predicted to be one of tomorrow's biggest stars. "Every year a few names explode from the anxious pack to take on the faces, futures and profit percentages of a special category in which influential film makers are keenly interested: Hollywood's fastest rising stars," wrote Martin Kasindorf in his article.

He went on to describe River as "the Designated Kid which appeals to the 15 to 25-year-olds while attracting the interest of older ticket buyers. Currently the busiest teenage star is fast-growing River Phoenix."

River had accomplished more in eight years than other actors even dream about. He managed to prove his talents to the show-business world and win the hearts of moviegoers at the same time. River is one of the most popular teenage actors on-screen today and he is prepared for all that Hollywood has to offer him in the years ahead. He's learned, in the past, to take the good with the bad and hasn't let either stand in his way of achieving success. He certainly possesses the insight and natural ability to keep his career prospering for many years to come.

River, however, doesn't think about the future. He likes to take things one day at a time. "Everything relies on time," he says. "There will be some of us (teenage actors) who will grow up and maybe stay in acting. Then others will want to do other things. I love how things happen!"

For River, things are happening very fast. With a music career about to take shape, River envisions this as his main goal. His bedroom is filled with a collection of instruments including six guitars, electric keyboards, bongos, and a bass guitar—obviously the sign of a serious musician. He has an album on the way, and as his fans eagerly await its release, they are beginning to wonder what kind of songs he writes.

"My music is original," he says. "Some of it is rock and some is mellow. I guess you could say it's rock with a touch of new wave and pop, but it branches off." One thing you can be sure of: River Phoenix writes from the heart.

"I usually like the words to rhyme," he explains. "But I did write a song once called 'Attic Window' where there were no rhymes at all."

It is a strong possibility that music will never take over River's career completely. He readily admits he'd like to get involved with many different aspects of show business. If he woke up one morning and found that he was no longer an actor, River would simply go on to whatever else interested him. He has said that he admires directors and would someday love to have the opportunity to direct a film.

"A director can just sit back and observe people," says River. "I'd feel more comfortable doing that than being observed. It's something that I've often thought about going into."

Bright, versatile, free-spirited River Phoenix seems to be enjoying his success even though it took him a while to adjust to his celebrity status. He knows the pitfalls of the business: One day you could rise to the top; the next you could fall.

"I know there are a lot of negative people in show business," he admits. "But I'm not going to be judgmental. One of the hardest things in life is to try to find a definition of yourself. If somebody has found one that I don't agree with, then I'm not going to say anything bad about them. At least they've made the first step."

For many young actors who suddenly find themselves at the top, the toughest task is keeping everything in perspective. River, it seems, is handling everything just fine. "One thing I don't have and never will have is an ego," he says. "That isn't the way I was brought up. I'm just like all the other kids in my family. We're real happy for this opportunity but don't think we're better than anyone else just because we act."

It is this easygoing attitude that appeals to so many of River's fans. While River Phoenix is soaring to new heights of stardom, he is remaining unchanged by all the hoopla. He is, quite frankly, a regular teenager. He can relate to his fans and they can relate to him.

How does River, who has such a bright future ahead of him, stay so level-headed? His answer is quick, stern, and sensible. "I just look in the mirror and say to myself, 'I see you. I know who you really are,' " he says.

Will River be an actor in the future? A singer? Director? Instead of giving a definite answer, he wants to keep his future open to anything that comes along. One thing that is certain: River will always be part of the entertainment world. He has had an enriching experience in show business and he appears to have a deep affection for and dedication to both acting and music.

It's not fame but work that is crucial to River. "I'm an actor, not a star," he says. "What I care about is being the best actor I can be. The bottom line is your talent. You've got to think work all the time. If stardom becomes your main concern, you could get swallowed up in a lot of bad values."

Despite River's strong protest against stardom, he remains at the top. It has already been predicted that when he gives up his crown as today's most popular teen hero and heartthrob, he will continue to shine as one of tomorrow's biggest and brightest stars.

Until that time comes, River Phoenix remains the most exciting young actor on the silver screen. And that's one title he is very proud of.

RIVER'S FACT FILE

FULL REAL NAME: River Jude Phoenix

NICKNAMES: Riv, Rio (Spanish for "river")

BIRTHDATE: August 23, 1970

BIRTHPLACE: Madras, Oregon

HEIGHT: 5'10½"

WEIGHT: 155 lbs.

HAIR COLOR: Dark blond

EYE COLOR: Blue-gray

FAMILY: Parents John and Arlyn, brother Leaf, sisters Rainbow, Liberty, and Summer

FIRST ACTING BREAK: River appeared in several commercials, but quit at age ten because he didn't like the idea of promoting products he didn't believe in.

FAVORITES

COLOR: Blue

CLOTHES: Jeans, T-shirts, and sneakers. He prefers darker colors and nothing too trendy.

FOOD: Vegetarian and Chinese dishes, mangoes, coconuts, and oranges

DRINK: Orange juice

ACTORS: Robert DeNiro, Anthony Michael Hall, Warren Beatty

MOVIE: *Brazil*

BOOK: *Siddhartha,* by Hermann Hesse

SUBJECTS: Geometry and literature

PLACE: The beach

INSTRUMENTS PLAYED: Guitar, bass, keyboards

IDEAL GIRL: Someone nice. "That's what attracts me," he says.

BEST FRIENDS: Dweezil and Moon Zappa, Wil Wheaton

GIRLFRIEND: He has dated Martha Plimpton, who co-starred with him in *The Mosquito Coast* and *Running On Empty*.

PET PEEVES: Being treated differently because he's an actor, and being in a cramped space with people who smoke

PASTIMES: Playing guitar, writing songs and poetry, going on family outings

PETS: Two dogs named Justice and Sundance

ULTIMATE FANTASY: World peace

FUTURE PLANS: River wants to continue acting, but is pursuing a career in music as well. He also wants to become a director someday.

WHERE TO WRITE TO RIVER: River Phoenix
c/o Columbia Pictures
711 Fifth Avenue
New York, NY 10022

RIVER SPEAKS OUT

On Success

"I'm just a normal guy doing a job!"

"After *Stand By Me* came out people were telling me, 'You're so good,' 'You're going to be a star,' and things like that. You can't think about it. If you take it the wrong way, you can get really high on yourself. People get so lost when that happens to them. They may think they have everything under control, but everything is really out of control. Their lives are totally in pieces."

On His Childhood Experiences

"We were constantly moving to different countries and adjusting to new things. It was such a free feeling. I'm glad I didn't have a traditional upbringing."

On Himself

"That's tough. Let's see—I can't tell a joke, that's for sure, and I'm moody sometimes. But I think I'm a good guy. I mean I know how not to rub people the wrong way."

"I'm really normal. I play football, go to the beach, drive. We have dogs. I can imagine other people calling me a character, but I'm Joe Straight."

On Quitting Commercials At Age Ten

"Commercials were too phony for me. I just didn't like selling a product I didn't believe in."

On Breaking Into Music

"I've been wanting to go into music ever since I can remember. I mean even before I became an actor. I just thought it would be a tough field to break into, so I became an actor instead."

"Music is my main goal, but I'm not going to rush a record out. There are so many actors who have come out with albums these days. I don't want to do it just because it's the thing to do. I want to wait until the time is right."

On Acting

"Acting is like a Halloween mask that you put on."

On *Stand By Me*

"I didn't expect it to be the hit it has become. But it was a great production. I wasn't surprised that it came out so well. I thought our director, Rob Reiner, was the best. Plus I made friends with Wil Wheaton, Corey Feldman, and Jerry O'Connell. I think that we'll always remain good friends, just like our characters in the movie."

On *The Mosquito Coast*

"I did my best work in *The Mosquito Coast*. I know it wasn't such a big hit, but for me it was more meaningful than anything else I'd ever done."

On Girls

"I like girls who are natural because I am natural in everything I do. If I meet a girl who is really snobby and wants special treatment, she's not going to get it from me because she hasn't earned it. But I've been basically lucky because I've met mostly nice girls—and that's what attracts me."

On His Fans

"It's a great feeling to think that I can be a friend to so many people through my movies."

On His Character In *A Night in the Life of Jimmy Reardon*

"Jimmy is like a junior-league Don Juan. He is more manipulative than I am and bolder with women."

On His Family

"People wonder if I'll always be part of this family and the answer is yes. My family has a lot of good energy going in one direction and because of it, we get a lot of things done. That's why I'll always spend a lot of time at Camp Phoenix."

On His Future

"I'd like to play every type of character, but only once. I like to experience things."

"I would never, never do anything unless I believed in it."

RIVER FILMOGRAPHY

EXPLORERS (1985)

DIRECTED BY: Joe Dante
EXECUTIVE PRODUCER: Mike Finnell
PRODUCED BY: Edward S. Feldman, David Bombyk
SCREENPLAY BY: Eric Luke
SPECIAL MAKEUP EFFECTS BY: Rob Bottin
MUSIC BY: Jerry Goldsmith
RELEASED BY: Paramount Pictures

Ben Crandall . . . . Ethan Hawke
Wolfgang Muller . . . . River Phoenix
Darren Woods . . . . Jason Presson
Lori Swenson . . . . Amanda Peterson
Charlie Drake . . . . Dick Miller

STAND BY ME (1986)

DIRECTED BY: Rob Reiner
PRODUCED BY: Andrew Scheinman, Bruce A. Evans, Raynold Gideon

SCREENPLAY BY: Raynold Gideon and Bruce A. Evans
BASED ON: "The Body" by Stephen King
DIRECTOR OF PHOTOGRAPHY: Thomas del Ruth
EDITOR: Robert Leighton
ORIGINAL MUSIC BY: Jack Nitzsche
RELEASED BY: Columbia Pictures

Gordie Lachance	Wil Wheaton
Chris Chambers	River Phoenix
Teddy DuChamp	Corey Feldman
Vern Tessio	Jerry O'Connell
Gordie Lachance (adult)	Richard Dreyfuss
Ace Merrill	Kiefer Sutherland
Eyeballs Chambers	Bradley Gregg
Billy Tessio	Casey Siemaszko

THE MOSQUITO COAST (1986)

DIRECTED BY: Peter Weir
PRODUCED BY: Jerome Hellman
SCREENPLAY BY: Paul Schrader
FROM THE NOVEL BY: Paul Theroux
EXECUTIVE PRODUCER: Saul Zaentz
MUSIC BY: Maurice Jarre
DIRECTOR OF PHOTOGRAPHY: John Seale, A.C.S.
EDITED BY: Thom Noble
RELEASED BY: Warner Brothers

Allie Fox	Harrison Ford
Mother	Helen Mirren
Charlie Fox	River Phoenix
Jerry Fox	Jadrien Steele
April Fox	Hilary Gordon

Clover Fox . . . . Rebecca Gordon
Emily Spellgood . . . . Martha Plimpton

A NIGHT IN THE LIFE OF JIMMY REARDON (1988)

WRITTEN AND DIRECTED BY: William Richert
FROM THE NOVEL: *Aren't You Ever Gonna Kiss Me Goodbye?*
   by William Richert
EXECUTIVE PRODUCERS: Mel Klein, Noel Marshall
PRODUCED BY: Russell Schwartz, Richard H. Prince
MUSIC BY: Bill Conti
DIRECTOR OF PHOTOGRAPHY: John J. Connor
EDITOR: Suzanne Fenn
RELEASED BY: 20th Century Fox Film Corporation

Jimmy Reardon . . . . River Phoenix
Joyce Fickett . . . . Ann Magnuson
Lisa Bentwright . . . . Meredith Salenger
Denise Hunter . . . . Ione Skye
Suzie Middleberg . . . . Louanne
Fred Roberts . . . . Matthew L. Perry
Al Reardon . . . . Paul Koslo
Faye Reardon . . . . Jane Hallaren

LITTLE NIKITA (1988)

DIRECTED BY: Richard Benjamin
PRODUCED BY: Harry Gittes
COPRODUCED BY: Art Levinson
SCREENPLAY BY: John Hill and Bo Goldman
STORY BY: Tom Musca and Terry Schwartz
DIRECTOR OF PHOTOGRAPHY: Laszlo Kovacs, A.S.C.
MUSIC BY: Marvin Hamlisch

EDITED BY: Jacqueline Cambas
PRODUCTION DESIGNED BY: Gene Callahan
RELEASED BY: Columbia Pictures

Roy Parmenter . . . . Sidney Poitier
Jeff Grant . . . . River Phoenix
Richard Grant . . . . Richard Jenkins
Elizabeth Grant . . . . Caroline Kava
Konstantin Karpov . . . . . . Richard Bradford
Scuba . . . . Richard Lynch
Verna McLaughlin . . . . Loretta Devine
Barbara Kerry . . . . Lucy Deakins

RUNNING ON EMPTY (1988)

DIRECTED BY: Sidney Lumet
PRODUCED BY: Griffin Dunne and Amy Robinson
SCREENPLAY BY: Naomi Foner
PRODUCTION DESIGN: Philip Rosenberg
EDITED BY: Andy Mondshein
RELEASED BY: Lorimar Film Entertainment

CAST: River Phoenix, Judd Hirsch, Christine Lahti, Martha Plimpton

TELEVISION APPEARANCES

Television Commercials for Ocean Spray, Mitsubishi, Saks Fifth Avenue
Fantasy (guest appearance)
Seven Brides for Seven Brothers (TV series. River played Guthrie)
Celebrity (TV miniseries)
Robert Kennedy: The Man and His Times (TV miniseries. River played Robert Kennedy as a boy)

Backwards: The Riddle of Dyslexia (ABC Afterschool Special. River played Brian Ellsworth)
Surviving: A Family in Crisis (TV movie)
Family Ties (guest appearance)
It's Your Move (guest appearance)
Hotel (guest appearance)
Circle of Violence: A Family Drama (TV movie. River played Chris Benfield)